From Jim and
Heather On my 85 th
birthday. May 26, 1984.

EAST AND WEST

EAST AND WEST

Selected Poems of

GEORGE FALUDY

Edited by John Robert Colombo

With a Profile of the Poet by Barbara Amiel

Hounslow Press

Toronto

ISBN 0-88882-025-9

Printed in Canada.

Designer: Susana Wald
Medallions: Dora de Pédery Hunt
Typesetter: Blain Berdan
Printer: Porcupine's Quill, Inc.

Publisher:

Hounslow Press,
124 Parkview Avenue,
Toronto M2N 3Y5,
Ontario, Canada

Translators

John Robert Colombo
R.G. Everson
Andrew Faludy
Eric Johnson
George Jonas
Dennis Lee
Gwendolyn MacEwen
Raymond Souster
Kathleen Szasz
Stephen Vizinczey
J. Michael Yates

A number of these translations have previously appeared in periodicals, anthologies, and individual volumes of verse. "You Should Know Something about George Faludy" by Barbara Amiel is reprinted in a slightly revised form from *Saturday Night,* December, 1973.

The author and the publisher wish to acknowledge grants received from the Canada Council and the Ontario Arts Council which assisted in the writing of these poems and the publishing of this collection.

Contents

You Should Know Something about George Faludy
By Barbara Amiel

Budapest, 1950: After forty-two days George Faludy has mastered life in prison. His cell contains a board to sleep on, half an inch of water on the floor and fungus on the walls. The rules are simple. It is forbidden to sit during the day. He is allowed to urinate once every twenty-four hours. Once or twice a week, late at night, he hears a familiar sequence of sounds: the flat noise of an unresisting body being dragged along the corridor; the sound as it tumbles into liquid, then the brief torn howl. Seconds later the smell of acid fills his cell. Later Faludy returns to his work. Pacing the narrow cell, privation and pain recede as his imagination seizes on remembered images of the outside world. In the windowless basement of the Secret Police headquarters, George Faludy plays with hexameters and metaphors. Poetry created without pen, paper or freedom. Fifty lines of poetry to be created and memorized by nightfall.

The new interrogator wears knickerbockers and shiny boots. "Puss-in-boots," thinks Faludy. The questioning begins with an energetic series of kicks to Faludy's groin, well placed by the bright leather boots. At noon there is a two-hour pause for lunch. Faludy waits as instructed, motionless, standing with his nose pushed against the wall, his body drenched in perspiration. Puss-in-boots returns in an excellent mood. He gives Faludy back half of one of the American cigarettes that were taken from him at the time of his arrest. He has a favour to ask: it concerns some poetry written by his nephew that he would like Faludy to read. Faludy is taken to a clean cell and given dinner. There are cakes and grapes and good black coffee. After dinner he reads the poetry. He knows that the seventy poems are in fact written by Puss-in-boots himself and he notes with some relief that they contain no evidence of talent.

Monday morning's interrogation begins with a show of excessive politeness. Faludy is invited to sit in a chair while, in a state of some excitement, Puss-in-boots asks about the poetry. Faludy savours the situation for a moment and then, as he later related in his autobiography *My Happy Days in Hell*: ". . . Very clearly and in great detail, I explained to him the aim and meaning of poetry. . . . I asked him to tell his nephew, as tactfully as possible, that he was writing decadent, rotten, reactionary poems of Western orientation. I begged him solemnly to forgive his nephew. . . . He would never, under any circumstances, become a poet and a Communist society must fight with every means at its disposal against such dilettantism. I had decided to tell him the truth while still in my cell, because apart from any utilitarian consideration I hated dilettantes even worse than AVO [secret police] men."

Toronto, 1973: In an attic room, only a little larger than the cell on Andrassy Street in Budapest, George Faludy sits drinking clear tea and smoking his fifteenth (whole) cigarette of the evening. He lives here in a room freshly painted, scrupulously clean and bare except for hundreds of books and a typewriter. At sixty he has white hair, a lined face and the eyes of a young man. Next to the typewriter is the completed manuscript of his new book, *The History of Humanism*. An immense work, it has absorbed him for the past two years. Three years ago his book *Erasmus of Rotterdam*, also written in Toronto and published in London and New York, received wide critical acclaim. In its review, the *Times* of London described the book as an example of Faludy's "typical combination of good, first-hand scholarship, with a sense of the overwhelming irony implicit in the subsequent history of humanism." In London, New York, Copenhagen and Vienna, George Faludy has a name of distinction. In Canada, he is virtually unknown.

Budapest, 1937: George Faludy walks on Nagykorut, the broad main street of Budapest. He is in his twenties. Streetcar conductors recognize him, sophisticated women and young girls smile invitingly to him. Culture is fashionable in Budapest the way cricket and pernod are fashionable in other capitals. Budapest still sees itself as the outpost of European culture and here the espresso-sipping housewife will sooner confess to an ignorance of couture than to an unfamiliarity with Anatole France. And George Faludy, in spite of his youth, is culture. His translations of the poems of François Villon, the fifteenth-century French poet, have taken Hungary by storm. Never mind, as the writer George Mikes is later to point out in the London Sunday *Times*, that Faludy's "translations" have very little to do with Villon. Faludy's poetry is exquisite and original and is read as much by the *littérateurs* sitting at the New York Café on Nagykorut St. as by the street bullies who will soon become the thugs of the Hungarian Nazi Arrow Cross Party and then, bowing to the needs of history, reinstate themselves as the Puss-in-boots' of the Communist terror.

Black coffee in front of him, friends next to him, Faludy sits with some satisfaction at the New York Café. He is blessed with fame, startling good looks and youth. But there is iron in his soul. His parlour skills as *raconteur* continue: he still dazzles friends with the ease with which he can parade twenty improvised rhymes, each more superbly wrought than the last, and in his modest apartment he shyly entertains yet another soft-eyed, smooth-skinned woman. But it is 1937 and he is also a member of the Social Democratic Party and an outspoken critic of fascism. As Hitler moves across Europe and Hungarian intellectuals move across Andrassy Street to apply for membership in the Nazi Arrow Cross Party, Faludy's actions become more dangerous. In Hungary, outspoken anti-fascists are few. Faludy's newspaper articles and poetry become increasingly sharp. His stand against the Nazis is without compromise. Later in England the critic Philip Toynbee will write: "The masters of the European hells never discarded a potential victim on the grounds that he wasn't suited to the role. Faludy may have been a lightweight, born for love and love songs, brilliant conversation, charming friendships, good food, good drink and an easy goodness of heart. He was also a brave and honourable man, and a poet with a dangerously high reputation."

Toronto, 1973: The Canadian Broadcasting Corporation's Studio Seven is the pride of the CBC television complex. In one corner of the darkened control room George Faludy peers over the banks of colour VTR monitors at the studio floor far below, where the actor Barry Morse is rehearsing the poem "Ave Luna, Morituri Te Salutant," written by Faludy. The poem is largely autobiographical and uses the first manned landing on the moon as a reference point for a passionate commentary on the ethics of man. Faludy is entranced by the technical gadgetry about him. He is aching to push a button, punch a dial. He is disbelieving: this crew of technicians, that group of actors, the disembodied voices on the intercom: is it possible they are all concerned with the production of his poem? On the literary black market his books of poetry have reached as many as twenty-seven editions. Now he turns to a Canadian friend standing next to him in the control room and whispers, "It is wonderful. And are they really going to do it on the cameras?"

Barry Morse is reading the poetry. Faludy is spellbound by the performance. Morse walks into the stark set: *"Seven times seven bars, doubled barbed wire,/and two more lines of barbed wire beyond/the window of the punishment cell. . . ."* Faludy is curiously moved by the pain and suffering Morse portrays. He seems to have forgotten the pain was his own.

Budapest, 1938: In the fashionable salons of Budapest the final pre-war parties are held. The passionate political harangues continue late into the night. George Faludy attends the parties. He has already been sentenced to a prison term and his case is being appealed in the courts. He is convicted of having vilified a friendly country, Germany. His accomplice in this seditious act is the German poet Heinrich Heine, who died in 1856, regarded Prussian military ambitions with some foreboding. Faludy translates Heine's *Germany,* including remarks like "Beware of the Germans" and "Should you hear a large bang the Germans will be behind it." Faludy is a faithful translator of Heine. The translation is published in Transylvania. Underground copies find their way to Budapest. Faludy's prison sentence is four years.

Not content to rely on the auguries of Heine, Faludy composes anti-Nazi poetry of his own. His masterpiece is a polemic against a Hungarian Nazi leader, Andras Csillery, who attended Hitler's Nuremberg Congress. The poem is vituperative and accurate. Faludy knows his victim. In a class-conscious country he celebrates the mortality of Csillery, the longevity of the written word and particularly this poem, which will record forever that not only did Csillery sell his country to the Germans but that he was after all only a miserable dentist. Upon seeing the illegally printed poem, Csillery has a heart attack. Faludy receives an additional two-year prison sentence.

But the etiquette of the Court, the *politesse* on which Hungarian society thrived, lingers yet. While Faludy is still outside prison awaiting his final appeal, he receives a phone call from the Hungarian Under Secretary of Justice. Politely the official explains that he has in his desk drawer a warrant of arrest for Faludy. This is most distressing to him, particularly since his wife had hoped for an autographed edition of Faludy's poetry. The Under Secretary wonders if it would be convenient for Faludy to "leave" Hungary, prison conditions being what they are at this time. Would it further be possible for Mr. Faludy to send him a postcard from Paris of the Paris Opera House? Upon receipt of such a postcard the Minister would take the warrant out of his desk drawer and have it executed. Within three weeks the official's wife has a signed edition of the poetry of the political fugitive George Faludy on a table next to her bed. On the desk of the Under Secretary of Justice is a postcard of the Paris Opera House. In Hungary the Nazis will burn George Faludy's books and deprive him of Hungarian nationality. In 1938, Faludy arrives in Paris confident that here the fight against the Nazis will be successful.

New York, 1945: He knows now. The grim details of events in Budapest reach Faludy in New York in a letter forwarded to him through the American legation in Budapest. For three months Budapest was under siege, the city without food. The Nazis, occupying the city in face of hopeless odds, prefer to sacrifice the civilian population rather than surrender. In the last vicious months of 1944, Faludy's sister, a doctor of medicine, is seized by the Nazis, shot, and thrown into the Danube. His father, unable to survive without food and medicine, dies too. Most of Faludy's friends have been shot or taken to camps.

Now the cry is for trials of the German war criminals. In New York Faludy joins the list of prominent intellectuals who object to the trials: Reinhold Niebuhr, G.A. Borgese, Carlo Sforza. The columns of the *Nation* and the newspapers are filled with the debate. Faludy takes a strong stand against the Nuremberg trials. His dilemma is that of a man whose moral sense is in advance of his other senses. His emotions are directed by his morality and he cannot equate his desires with what he feels is right. For Faludy, all who acquiesced in Hitler's rise to power — including the industrialists of America and Great Britain — should be on trial. It is also inconceivable to Faludy that the victor can be the *judge* of the vanquished. You take revenge on a defeated enemy, but you cannot be prosecutor, judge and jury. (Later he opposes the Eichmann trial on similar grounds. How can the victims try the murderer?) But now sentiment peaks for the Nuremberg trials. To be pro-trial is to be pro-justice. Faludy wishes to kill the beast. But he cannot stand silent and watch the concept of justice killed at the same time. The left wing and anti-fascists consider him a reactionary.

Toronto, 1969: The University of Toronto campus is bleak. Students wrapped in scarves and heavy coats crossing the icy windswept grounds between Convocation Hall and University College are concerned with the approaching spring exams and ignore the delegation of right-wing Hungarians who have come to protest the lectures of George Faludy. The University of Toronto and some members of the Toronto Hungarian community have contributed equal funds to enable Faludy to give a short series of lectures one evening a week.

The delegation crossing the campus to protest Faludy's lectures is a motley group, but to a student of Hangarian society they are recognizable. In pre-war Hungary some minority groups, such as the Schwabs, the Saxons and the Jews, were successful in numbers disproportionate to their population. These groups were resented by extreme nationalists, populists, facists and the petit intelligentsia. Their resentment hardened when a minority group member joined one of the left-wing political parties, such as the Social Democrats. When the war made a mockery of their nationalism and turned them into exiles from their homeland, some came to Canada. Now, once again, as they cross the University of Toronto campus, their resentment is exacerbated. George Faludy — Social Democrat and successful writer — is to have a university appointment while their own poets work as janitors and tradesmen.

Dean Ernest Sirluck receives many letters, mostly unsigned, labelling George Faludy a "godless, atheistic Communist." Leaflets written in Hungarian are strewn on the campus and Sirluck has them translated. What the anonymous English letters leave unsaid, the Hungarian pamphlets spell out: gutter rhetoric, including denunciations of Faludy as a Jew. Sirluck has security guards posted at Faludy's lectures. He is appalled by the campaign, impressed by Faludy, and not at all intimidated by what he refers to as "a nasty, dirty protest." Dean Sirluck, his budget overspent, has found the money for Faludy's lectures out of contingency funds. The short series of lectures ends that spring and is not continued in the fall. (In 1973, Ernest Sirluck, now president of the University of Manitoba, will ask an interviewer: "What happened to George Faludy?")

Morocco, 1941: On the marble table under the hand-carved cedar wood beams of the house in Marrakesh is a large stiff envelope addressed to George Faludy. President Franklin Roosevelt suggests that Mr. Faludy come to America "where he could continue his valuable work in peace and security until the end of the war." The invitation pleases Faludy enormously. He has escaped the Nazis by a hairbreadth, first in Hungary, then in France. Now the Gestapo is in Morocco. Unfortunately, Roosevelt's letter, impressive as it is on the stiff shiny paper with the embossed seal, does not solve his immediate problem. Faludy has nothing but his expired Hungarian passport to carry him across the borders between Morocco and America, and in time of war border guards often fall victim to attacks of conscientiousness that result in the incorruptible scrutiny of papers. The Imperial House of Hapsburg comes to the rescue. In Marrakesh is the Hotel Hungaria, which has adopted the emblem of the Austro-Hungarian empire as its motif. With the aid of Hungarian ingenuity, Arab stealth and a hard boiled egg (by means of which the Hapsburg emblem is transferred from the hotel's seal), Faludy's passport is soon stamped with the double eagle of the House of Hapsburg. It will intimidate any border guard.

New York, 1941: As the ship carrying Faludy steams into New York harbour, the distinguished Hungarians gathered to greet him glance nervously at their welcoming speeches. An article in the New York *Post* about Faludy is sent up to the ship in care of a sailor. It is a sunny, misty afternoon. Roosevelt's letter of invitation to America is in Faludy's pocket. The U.S. immigration officials are polite but firm. Letter or not, Faludy will not be permitted to land. He has no U.S. visa. He will be detained on Ellis Island. It has further come to the officials' attention that Faludy is an active anti-fascist, which is premature — for America the war hasn't started yet. Immigration attitudes are as unsympathetic to premature anti-fascists as they are to mature fascists. Faludy is on Ellis Island for one month. The newspapers have a field day: "Roosevelt's Guest Interned on Ellis Island." For Faludy there are interesting aspects to his situation. He is in a country where all are more or less equal before the law and even Roosevelt's guests need visas if they are to live and work in the United States. This consoles him.

Indiana, 1942: Wearing his American army uniform, Faludy sits a little nervously on the train. He has no idea where the train is going. Faludy is a conversationalist. He discovers that the soldiers on this train all seem to have come from those areas of Europe that once formed the Austro-Hungarian Empire. He is surrounded by Czechs, Hungarians, Italians, Austrians and Slovaks. It is, he decides, an example of naive American thoughtfulness. Faludy sleeps. His dreams contain a recurring nightmare. He is pursued by the Nazis. They have tied him to a tree and are about to torture him. The train suddenly stops. A voice wakens Faludy with the words *"Aussteigen!"* (get out). It is no nightmare. George Faludy has been recruited for the infamous "Hapsburg Legion."

An American State Department fantasy, the Hapsburg Legion (officially known as the 101st Infantry Battalion Separate) is born of a flirtation between Otto of Hapsburg and Secretary of War Henry Stimson. It will have no artillery but will provide an escort for Otto. Faludy finds himself wearing a small black and gold insignia on his American uniform. German lessons are part of basic training at the Indiana camp, where plans are in high gear to train the men in the decorum necessary for a battalion whose leader has never renounced his claim to the throne of the Austro-Hungarian Empire. The Hapsburg Legion is short-lived. Faludy joins those signing petitions in the New York *Times* and other papers to end this farce. The *Nation* writes derisively of "Otto's Freikorps." Faludy is transferred by the army to Palo Alto, Calif., where he teaches French and German history to men who are being prepared to take over European industry and commerce when American occupation begins in earnest at the end of the war. The army has taken over a fraternity building to house its staff in Palo Alto.

Faludy discovers that in the U.S. Army he is expected to leave his boots outside the door each night to be cleaned. Later, as a tail gunner flying over Japan, it becomes evident that even in the relative comfort of the American Air Force, war is still a matter of blood and dirt.

When the war ends Faludy must decide whether to return to Hungary. Feelings of nostalgia and genuine terror complicate the decision. Brutality, doublethink and the loss of freedom are the realities he has left behind once. But his books, seized, banned and burned by the Nazis, are now being published again. Hungary's liberal newspapers are calling for his return. For Faludy the question of whether democracy or dictatorship will triumph in Hungary is crucial. He cannot afford to sit and watch in America.

Budapest, 1949: It is the birthday of Comrade Matyas Rakosi, the Stalinist boss of Hungary. His birthday is celebrated with laudatory articles and poems in all the papers. George Faludy writes nothing. A perspiring and eager Undersecretary of Culture visits Faludy to express the regret felt in party circles at this omission. Such an omission lends credence to the rumours that Faludy is a reactionary monarchist with fascist friends in America. After the Undersecretary leaves, Faludy smokes an American cigarette and decides not to write a poem. This is the final straw. Faludy has declined invitations to join the Communist Party. He has refused propaganda work and shown no interest in helping the party as an informer. He has clung with stubbornness to literary forms that social realism has made obsolete. He has been seen to have a copy of the works of Edgar Allan Poe. Six days later he is arrested.

After three days in the prison at 60 Andrassy Street a young lieutenant comes to Faludy with paper, pencils and cigarettes. He assures Faludy that he will be out of prison the next day if he will only write the poem. Faludy thanks him and refuses. "The angels come before they beat you to death. I am not in prison to write poems to Rakosi." The nice young lieutenant goes out of the cell. He leaves the pack of cigarettes behind.

Faludy is sent to a concentration camp at Recsk. There the whispered lectures he gives at night in philosophy, literature and the culture of the Greek, Byzantium and Renaissance periods help sustain the spiritual and intellectual life of the starving, tortured men. On March 5, 1953, Joseph Stalin dies. In the brief, breast-beating period that follows, the camp is closed, saving those inmates who have managed to survive the brutality. Faludy survives because of his own moral strength and ingenuity and because his fellow prisoners have made his survival their priority.

Toronto, 1973:   In an apartment in North Toronto a group of Hungarians gather. Most of them are Canadian citizens now. They are taxi drivers, engineers, stagehands, accountants. For a few years in the early 1950s they lived together in the camp at Recsk. Many of them were survivors of the Nazi concentration camps. At Recsk, the concentration camp of the Communists, they found the methods similar, the ideology substantially the same. Only the vocabulary differed. In the small apartment in North Toronto they surround George Faludy as they did in the camp. For the few Canadians present, Faludy explains why he could not simply write a poem for Rakosi. "First you must understand Rakosi had no neck. His head came straight out of his shoulders. He was bald. There are good bald men. This was a vile bald man. How could I write a good poem about a vile man? It could be done in the Renaissance when there were tyrants everywhere. You could even do it of Stalin, who had stature in his monstrosity." Rakosi, like many Hungarian Communists of the old guard, had a fairly decent education. He could recognize a badly written poem. It would have been useless for Faludy to have simply written a poem. The poem had to be good. "So you see," Faludy explains, "my act of refusal only *looked* like a moral act."

Budapest, 1955: George Faludy is free and unemployed. No one is sure whether it is safe to hire him. The source of his problem lies on Academy Street, near Parliament Square, close to the Danube. On this street are a large number of government buildings. Here is the Ministry of the Interior. In a totalitarian country the Ministry of the Interior is the most important ministry. No one enters without an invitation. There is no general enquiry desk. There are no receptionists to point out the various offices or impatient switchboard operators to connect you with the right department. In fact, there is no available phone number. The doors have guards. Visitors have passes.

In order to employ George Faludy safely it must be established that he is in good standing with the Ministry of the Interior. But the very act of inquiring about an individual's status is heretical. To begin with, one should already know the answer. Furthermore, such an enquiry suggests the existence of a blacklist, which in a people's democracy is nonsense and such a notion may result in imprisonment. The Writers' Association is afraid to take Faludy back as a member and this makes it virtually impossible for him to obtain a job. Faludy's friends, however, solve the problem. It is brought to the attention of the Translators' Guild that George Faludy is fluent in Danish, Norwegian, Swedish, and Icelandic. This is useful because virtually nobody else in Hungary is. Faludy is accepted into the Translators' Guild. He does not speak these languages, but he does command a fluent German and Germans are conscientious translators: not only do they translate everything, they translate word for word. Faludy earns a living by translating German translations of Danish, Norwegian, Swedish and Icelandic books into Hungarian. Everyone is satisfied.

Toronto, 1973: On the nineteenth floor of a luxurious apartment building, a party is being held. The couch is down-filled dark green corduroy. Under a real mimosa tree surrounded by actors, pickled exotica and glasses of Scotch, sits George Faludy. The party is in honour of the CBC production of Faludy's poem. Barry Morse and his wife strain to hear Faludy against the rising din. Faludy is not at ease. He loves conversation. He will sit up all night to talk of Socrates or Maimonides. His small talk is witty and elegant. But the crush of too many bodies in a small room and shrill voices that render all conversation cacophonous are too much for him. He escapes into the bedroom.

In the hallway a slightly drunk actor asks him why he left Hungary in 1956. The actor is a member of the New Left. Faludy replies that he was tired. He had waited for freedom too long. The worst thing in life, Faludy explains, is to see things and have to remain silent. The actor is persistent. But why Canada, he asks, why did you come to Canada?

Vienna, 1956: The streets are full of Hungarians. Two hundred and fifty thousand of them have crossed the border. You can tell them at a glance by the East European clothes showing the effects of hiding in marshes or jumping barbed wire. The refugees gather in the elegant Café Europe; exile has not compromised their taste in espresso or altered their perception of social strata. The talk is of future plans. To which country are you going?

George Faludy, like his fellow refugees, has no valid passport, a familiar situation for him. The Austrians have given the refugees stateless Austrian papers. Valid papers will require patience and a waiting period of some time. Faludy's papers arrive promptly. He and his wife are given Costa Rican passports fully accredited and issued in San José. They are delivered to Faludy in Vienna by a Costa Rican government emissary. The passports enable Faludy to accept the offer of a lecture tour of South America sponsored by a trade-union movement. The passports cause immigration officials in Costa Rica some bewilderment when, at the San José airport, it is discovered that George Faludy, native of Costa Rica, cannot speak a word of Spanish.

South America, 1957: Faludy's lectures on political theory and philosophy take him across South America. It is in Costa Rica that he discovers the advantages and personal disadvantages of a republic that has taken the concept of democracy very much to heart. Standing patiently ahead of him in line for a movie in San José is the President of Costa Rica. Such egalitarianism is impressive. But at the end of his visit, when Faludy comes to check out of the hotel in which he has stayed as a guest of the people of Costa Rica, he discovers that "guest" is an abstract term of courtesy and friendship in a small country where everyone is considered equal. He is expected to pay the full hotel bill. This discovery has repercussions for the duration of his South American travels. For the remainder of the trip he spurns the lavish hotels his hosts offer in favour of small boarding houses. Unable to dissuade his insistent hosts in Brazil, he and his wife are shown to a lavish suite in a luxury hotel in Rio de Janeiro. High up above the swimming pool in the air-conditioned splendour of their mosaic-tile suite, Faludy and his wife eat chunks of crusty bread over the bathtub to hide the crumbs, and drink nothing but water. This way they hope to be able to afford the hotel bill. After a stay of some length and their fill of bread and water they discover the bill has been paid in full by their hosts.

While on his lecture tour, Faludy learns that he has been deprived of his Hungarian nationality for the second time. On January 27, 1957, Prime Minister Janos Kadar goes to the Hungarian parliament to request the vote that will officially make Faludy a non-person. Janos Kadar, the old-line Communist who, like Faludy, was imprisoned under the Rakosi regime and is rumoured to have been emasculated while in jail, presides over the official demise of George Faludy. Now Faludy's books will be seized and banned as they were under the Nazis. The Communists will add the refinement of pulping them.

London, 1966: Here, among old friends, George Faludy has spent pleasant moments. He has stormed into the night after violent arguments with Arthur Koestler. He has argued till day-break with George Mikes. Such are the comforts of old friendships He has weathered certain disappointments. For four years he was editor-in-chief of the *Hungarian Literary Gazette,* published in London. The *Gazette* in Budapest was the official paper of the Hungarian Writers' Association and was the driving ideological force behind the 1956 revolution. Faludy discovers there are CIA pressures involved in its English publications and resists and is sacked. In London he has given dozens of talks on the BBC on literary matters. He has gone abroad to lecture at Universities in Sweden, Denmark and Iceland. (Those years in the Translators' Guild were not without value. Through the medium of German he gained an immense knowledge of Scandinavian literature.) It is in London that he writes his autobiography, *My Happy Days in Hell.* It is reprinted twice, becomes a book club selection, is translated into French, German, and Danish.

Now, after the jails, the concentration camp and exile, comes the heaviest blow. His wife dies of cancer after a three-year fight. Faludy flees London. He studies in Florence, Rome, and Venice, and finally stops in Malta. There he begins to write again.

Toronto, 1968: It has not been easy to get employment in Canada. Nobody knows George Faludy, though his books are in the public libraries and in some demand. (In fact it is virtually impossible to get a copy of *My Happy Days in Hell*. A touch of old Hungary: all circulating copies have been stolen.) He has a battered brown folder containing a few of his clippings, a single suitcase with two well-pressed suits and the odd shirt, his *curriculum vitae* and the cartons of books.

At Columbia University in New York City, Professor Robert P. Austerlitz hears through the academic grapevine that Faludy is back in North America. He invites him to Columbia for one guest lecture. At the end of the lecture he offers him a teaching position.

New York, 1968: Black militants stand easy in classroom doorways. Student radicals give the-way-it-is interviews to clusters of newsmen. It is the Columbia student strike. George Faludy walks quietly through the patrolled corridors, past the empty classrooms, in front of the revolutionaries. His students are not on strike. In the quadrangles of Columbia University, Faludy continues to give his lectures. When this becomes uncomfortable his students pack themselves into cars and drive to the home oɩ a friend of Faludy's in New Jersey. The lectures continue there till the strike is over.

Faludy brings the love of keen conversation and black coffee from the cafés of Vienna and Budapest to Amsterdam Street in New York City. There, in a small restaurant, he sits after lectures with his students. The coffee is more diluted than the dark cups he sipped in Budapest. But the crystal edge of Faludy's mind is not dulled. Luther, Aristotle, Orwell, Free Will or Iris Murdoch: the excitement of ideas and the incredible range of human achievement remained his strength in the concentration camp, his thread of sanity in solitary confinement, and now the continuity for a difficult existence in the New World.

Faludy teaches at Columbia for two years but insists on living in Toronto and commuting weekly to New York. According to American immigration regulations, Faludy — as a non-resident — can work only two years. Faludy is a natural teacher and Columbia decides to risk the third year. Laurentian University at Sudbury, Ontario, advertises for a lecturer in Renaissance studies. Faludy, hoping to teach in Canada, sends them his book on Erasmus, his *curriculum vitae* and the names of several referees. The letter he receives is most appreciative. He is assured of a job the next year. There is no further communication.

Toronto, 1973: George Faludy packs the last of his books in cartons. He is leaving his rooms and moving in with friends. He does this with regret but it's necessary, at least till *The History of Humanism* is published. In the last two years he has been invited to Wesleyan University, the University of Buffalo, the University of Chicago, Rutgers, Princeton and numerous symposiums. But such lectures provide very little money. And he wishes to live in Canada.

The slight figure walks down the main street of Toronto. His eyes dart with curiosity at his fellow pedestrians. Eyes that know the death camps of Europe as well as the splendours of the Renaissance. His mind plays with the prose he has re-read that morning — Latin translations of Aristotle. He is the sort of man — in Philip Toynbee's words — all of us would like to be, as well as being ourselves.

Almost nobody in Canada knows George Faludy. But for some curious reason, George Faludy seems to believe that Canada is the right country for him.

Michelangelo's Final Sonnet

Earth is your anvil. You lord it over the sky,
and your arm sweeps like the sun's semi-circle.
For eighty-six years I crouched on my scaffold
without once finding you aloft, my Lord.

Marble, under my chisel's tip, crumbles into dust,
and I am left with an idol or a torso in my hand.
Not once did I find you, O evanescent rainbow;
instead you glowed away within my marble blocks.

An old block of stone is what I have become,
with a hundred gouges, mute, rough, miserable,
but still some heavenly light glows within my soul.

How can I shed this prison of my body?
Should you find yourself able to love an old sinner,
hit me, divine sculptor. Your marble am I.

Florence, 1935

The Crossing

Deep ford, steep waterbed,
the silent girls cross it
with eyes accusing and sad
from rocky shores, their heavy clothes
hanging like sheets of lead.

But let the keen brooks turn lean:
with waist-high skirts aloft
and roving eyes in a dream
girls are golden thighs in silver water
crossing a summer stream.

Hungary, 1935
George Jonas

Danse Macabre

The Emperor held court. In his hair
seven stars made a diadem,
the Big Dipper turned in his navel,
kneeling slaves paid homage to him.
On his bronzed arm the disc of new moon
cast a silver sickle of light,
only a humble clown sat meekly
at the foot of his throne and cried.
"Why are you crying," he yelled, "my sword
can touch every man's heart, I must
own the whole earth. . . ." By night a skeleton
blew him away like a speck of dust.
—We played the tyrant one and all,
years flew like minutes to amaze us
by the spilt dewdrops of your blood
be merciful to us Prince Jesus.

At his gothic window the Doctor whined:
"Lord, on which one of these hills
is your magic nectar growing
that is said to cure all ills?"
And through the door an emaciated don
danced across the den with a stein
held in leaden fingers of bone
offering his colourless wine:
"Drink, this brew is euphorically cool,
dries every wound, makes all pain numb;
drink up, colleague, from this deep chalice
only the first drop stings your tongue."
—We were false experts one and all,
years flew like minutes to amaze us,
by the spilt dewdrops of your blood
be merciful to us Prince Jesus.

The Child stood at the rim of the well
in a torn shirt and a pair of clay-
coloured slippers, and looked at his own
face in the water that called him to play.
" . . . The moonmaiden will give you candy
by the bonnetful if you come
and we will play tag with the bullfrogs
by the light of the morning sun."
"I'm coming . . ." he said and the water of the well
reared a green snake on his swelling belly, while
Death took the clay-coloured slippers and put them
in front of his mother with a slimy smile.
—We played childish games one and all,
years flew like minutes to amaze us
by the spilt dewdrops of your blood
be merciful to us Prince Jesus.

At her cracked mirror sat the Harlot:
"My flood of hair's still red, but why
is it that no lovers, companions
call me, and old friends pass me by?
The lips of my lap are readily parted
my nipples are hard as diamonds still. . . ."
And grinning the last bridegroom approached her
stepping across the windowsill:
"Up, Daisy, up, come dance with me,
your dead lovers had gone to ruin,
let larvae spread their wedding feast
on the wilted purple of your groin."
—We twisted in lust one and all,
years flew like minutes to amaze us
by the spilt dewdrops of your blood
be merciful to us Prince Jesus.

Pitchblack midnight embraced the rooftops
an owl's screech pierced the misty cold
as the Banker began his journey
to bury deep his bloody gold.

Seven devils hiding behind Death
stood at the crossroads, intrepid;
and when he drew his sword the skeleton
whispered to him, "You see, stupid,
you hang on to your moneysack,
this iron spike gives you a clout
and you'll get buried, not your gold,
and who will ever dig you out?"
—We were grim peddlers one and all,
years flew like minutes to amaze us
by the spilt dewdrops of your blood
be merciful to us Prince Jesus.

The Lady sat in her gold boudoir
and shrieked in terror: "Too soon, too soon,"
but he had already embraced the fair
domes of her hips in his arms of doom,
"let me have one more languid kiss,
one more dress of pearls, one more vain,
easy, casual compliment
or only one more night of pain . . ."
but painting a circular stain on her breast
that grew, like cancer grows, lumpy and rough,
he heaved her white body on his back
and carried and carried and carried her off.
—We languished in sloth one and all,
years flew like minutes to amaze us
by the spilt dewdrops of your blood
be merciful to us Prince Jesus.

The Alchemist stood by his fire
and looked at his sands that had run out.
"God or devil, give me one more day,
my retorts are brimming at the mouth;
the great puzzle is hiding inside
the white flames of my kilns of clay:
just one more day will see it yielding,
I'll have it solved in one more day!"

"You will not," said the voice, "you will not."
And held him firmly while the test-
tubes blew up, with icy hands.
"You'll go to sleep now like the rest."
—We looked for answers one and all
years flew like minutes to amaze us
by the spilt dewdrops of your blood
be merciful to us Prince Jesus.

The bells of pestilence rang in the plague
in front of the cathedral of Reims,
and on a bubonic Easter Sunday
it shook the stout Bishop by the hands:
"I did compose this tune for you,
let's go, my Lord! I ring my bells,
be pope or prophet, priest or scholar,
who in the holy scripts excels;
be a bishop or heretic, whose
sole relics are his blackened bones:
say Mass below; I peel my laughter
from the chill belfries of the domes."
—We were hypocrites one and all,
years flew like minutes to amaze us
by the spilt dewdrops of your blood
be merciful to us Prince Jesus.

The old Peasant stood in the barnyard
by nightfall; he expected him.
His worn body commanded no price,
he knew Death and accepted him:
"Brother reaper, our land is poor
and nothing will increase the yield.
Take this body, it's good manure,
and dress it deep into the field."
He nodded and carried him slowly
and sowed him, sowed him, sowed him in
like farmers' hands sow in the new seed
or poppies blow in autumn's wind. . . .

—We go underground one and all
years fly like minutes to amaze us
by the spilt dewdrops of your blood
be merciful to us Prince Jesus.

Budapest, 1935
George Jonas

Belated Epitaph at Thasos

Theris who had to do his work himself,
who harvested in among the waves,
was a lowly fisherman, not a Persian king,
who in a dinghy, not a well-manned galleon,
upon the briny flow of the waves,
slaved to eat just like the seagulls.

So he struggled with the ocean,
by daylight green, blue, yellow, wine-dark,
sometimes dull-grey, or like old ivory,
by night black- or silver-coloured,
and with swollen eyes spied for the
seventieth time the ominous Arcturus.

The ocean, his rumpled wedding bed,
had so craftily requited his love
that no evil befell him while he worked,
but fate caught up with him in the old
of his age, in the quiet of his hut,
like a lamp the oil of which is sucked dry.

As he had no wives, relatives or children,
this grave was dug by his neighbours,
they spread grass across it, and honey,
when the sun set, clear and cerulean,
and as a sign of their love what they left
on top of it were their tears of lead.

Greece, 1935

The Letter With Which Walafridus Strabo
Submitted His Book on Horticulture
to Grimaldus, the Abbot of St. Gall, Around 830 A.D.

The book my messenger leaves at your gate
is modest for a gift, not in accord
with the merits of a spirit as ornate
as yours is, O my father in the Lord.
But it comes from a follower in the faith
whose eyes even now, while he marks these dots,
behold you in a rockgarden beneath
a small tree bearing yellow apricots
surrounded by the offspring of your soul,
your family, disciples, casting lots
to gather for his pleasure pale-green peaches
on whose white beard the stars of which he teaches
throw showerheads of light through tiny slots
under the autumn's ornamental glass.
There, in that garden, gentle father, gazing
over the irises and tiger-grass,
advanced in age but in strength still amazing,
untouched by ill-health, sloth, or gluttony,
read — which I boldly send you for appraising —
my brief commentary on botany.
Ponder it deeply, my modest creation,
tender me about it no lenient lies,
castigate its faults for my edification,
but if it merits some favour in your eyes
extol its virtues, O voice that fills the land
with tones of ringing brass in major keys,
for which Christ may place in your ancient hand
the olive branch of His eternal peace.

Switzerland, 1936
George Jonas

Song of The German Mercenaries

Oh, we are the German mercenaries,
whose skin is like some well-worn hide.
What do we care whether we march
up the mountain or across the plain,
murdering gentlemen, peasants or priests,
going to the gallows, doing it for fun?
Under the sky we slept for months,
the grass we harvested before our eyes,
the city of Breda we watched in flames,
we ran after girls who were barely ten.
Since we are the German mercenaries,
whose skin is like some well-worn hide.

Have you ever set eyes on an infant child
hounded to death by the palace guards?
Like this they pressed us into service,
they gave us armour, they gave us shirts,
floggings are what the lieutenant did.
Like this we grew up, here we are now,
we show no mercy to woman or child,
even tiny infants we put to the wall,
we enter your room and snore in your bed,
your house we burn down on top of your head.
Since we are the German mercenaries,
whose skin is like some well-worn hide.

Seven are the counties we devastated,
we scaled the Seven Hills of Rome,
we slogged right through the autumn's mud,
we bathed all summer long in blood,
we swam in winter through fields of snow,
we waded across the Meuse like rats,
we sweated south of the River Po,
we were driven to drinking melted snow,

we ate up the locusts in the desert,
horrible the curses hurled against us.
Because we are the German mercenaries,
whose skin is like some well-worn hide.

We know no father, we knew no mother,
we severed the tree trunks from their roots,
we poisoned the water we found in the wells,
whoever we served could afford us well.
Without giving so much as a greeting,
we smash the sides of barrels and kegs,
we are carting away your precious belongings,
we quickly make your daughter a whore.
Unless you say, "Thank you, oh so much,"
we beat out your brains beside your door.
Because we are the German mercenaries,
whose skin is like some well-worn hide.

The years go on and when we get old,
dozing on wooden benches like fools,
feet being gobbled up by the gout,
Frundsberg's Sword grown more heavy,
the lieutenant kicking us out of the army,
we drag ourselves from city to city
beseeching anybody with a little love
to drop us a tiny crust of bread,
and thus we reach the end of the line
where Beelzebub stands and now is asking:
Are *these* the German mercenaries,
whose skin is like some well-worn hide?

Oh, we are the German mercenaries,
whose skin is like some well-worn hide.
What do we care whether we march. . . .
(*Reprise*)

Budapest, 1937

I Am Reading Chinese Poetry

Over the man-made island, which you reach by the back of the tiger,
which circles the lake like a bridge, and out of the lilac waves,
softly and with symmetry, rises the pavillion,
it is all blue, all green, all purple porcelain.

Joyfully companions sip rice wine and filch passing pleasures,
their tunics the colour of peach blossoms, or the horizon of the
    evening sky,
the first one drinks his yellow wine, the second one muses lazily,
the third one drops his heavy head upon his chest and begins a poem.

Alas, in the lake, within which the bridge shimmers like a jade and
    crescent moon,
Observe the madness there, and the intoxication on the artists' brows,
observe how they shiver in their robes, see the pavillion upside-down,
it is all, all, all porcelain.

Budapest, 1937

Wife

Your eyes are still a youthful shade of blue,
though you tag along behind me like a shadow
up and down the halls of tacky hotels
　　　and hostile avenues.

What is there left to confess about myself,
omniscient room-mate, my taciturn secretary?
I have gotten as used to you as to sunshine
　　　and the world.

I have gotten as used to you as the skies,
and the light, the sharpest spice of summer,
and the gleam of blue bottles of wine
　　　and of apricots.

I have called out to you: Take care of me,
should the fear of death overtake me at night;
be up those stairs where fumes of nothingness rise;
　　　be the balustrade.

As I warm myself on your sleeping body,
I left the past like a light shawl
and toss it about us the way I do
　　　the distant future.

And I imagine that we have to lie
in the outer darkness, sound asleep,
stiff throughout eternity, our bones falling apart
　　　in the yellow clay.

Nations will flash by overhead, and our sleep will be
one-tenth, one-one-hundredth, one-one-thousandth
of this endless prison, the gates of which now
　　　lie open to us.

Once upon a time I cried out that it was a shame,

but now, secretly, I feel a great humility
though when I hear the tiptoe of your step,
    I do confess:

I have gotten used to things, have learned to love
this desperate future, and for you I will be
the sum of years through which, like some dirty old man,
    I age into death.

Paris, 1939

Morocco

Yesterday, I brought home carrots;
today they are ochre paint.
I watch the skin of thirty-year-old women
parch, and then the hairline cracks begin.
Before my eyes, in random vehement bursts
all things in Marrakesh go hurtling forward
towards the abrupt perfection of their own deaths.
The strict and cool geometry of night
welters and sags in the torture pit of the sun,
which sows and harvests rot.
All day I draw it deep inside my lungs,
intoxicating spice, and zigzag through the streets,
where every corner is sacred to offhand murder.
Death swarms here.
And if you're young, that makes you his special darling:
he enters the bed at climax,
he takes the next chair at meals.

Yet everything I used to love at home
is altered here, become so much
irrelevant window-dressing. Boring. Fake.
And what, back there, disgusted me — this
vicious, barbarous country —
is closer to final truth.

I didn't write this poem by myself.
I'm sitting very still. It pleases me
to feel the way my muse, the fear of death,
is peeling me, layer by layer, to the bone.

Morocco, 1940
Dennis Lee

Twilight

The she-ass passes by, her belly full of udders,
rather like a rooster hanging from its claws.
The sun has set: convex parentheses remain,
a nocturnal wall of light, tall, moon-like;
    then it collapses.

We are seven, reclining on the lawnchairs in the garden,
ghosts in burnooses appear and disappear on the street.
An evening's silence here, a heavenly peace up there,
only the soles of our stretched-out feet can sense
    London is burning up.

The abbot sits amid the gloom like a well-fed raven,
quoting Lucan — on justice — in Latin.
I, incommunicado, am like some adventurer
ever-denying his father, ever-blushing when
    we are face to face.

The moon glows as nakedly as the sun,
sweat of dying men streams down our chests.
Little glowworms put in their appearance,
orphans who sway their hundred candles
    underneath the trees.

In the silence, amid a thicket of tamarisks, we lie,
seven corpses, a stage set for some *Walpurgisnacht.*
Again and again I find myself repeating
to myself this crazy sentence which runs:
    The night is living like the day.

Thus I begin to talk aloud, to unburden myself,
shadows creep over us like moss upon a tree,
until the moment when I feel across my face
the South Wind, like the snort of a horse from
    the Stables of King Solomon.

Morocco, after the Fall of France, 1940

Moroccan Beggar Woman At The End Of The Bus Line

Against the stone villa's wall she crouches,
her back stiff. In the sockets of her eyes
flies stroll about and suck up the pus.
She remains as motionless as if she were
nursing her child. Her face is terracotta;
she is not old. In her lap relax her hands.
When she hears the sound of the approaching bus
she frightens the flies with a sudden start.
The mob of wealthy passengers descend;
she straightens up, her lips clenched tight.
She asks nothing at all. A spark
of human dignity burns deep within.

Morocco, 1940

Death of a Chleuch Dancer

(Chleuch dancers are dancing boys of the
Chleuch tribe in Morocco who are famous
for being stained blue)

I burst into the marketplace
in time to see his face. It was sulphur-yellow.
They were lifting him from the ground, for he was dead;
the man he had been unfaithful to
had murdered him. Two people were holding the killer,
three kicked him, and one came behind with the dagger.
The crowd began to follow.
And I was left alone in front of the blood, which
did not penetrate the dust, but lay and rippled.
And I called back many gentle words the dancer had spoken.
I remembered the smell of his body, wild honey it was.
And I thought of his bright blue hair, a banner and
pillow at night.
How should I
honour his bittersweet memory?
I sat in the dust, destroyed, beside his blood,
and beat the flies away.

Morocco, 1940
Dennis Lee

On the Tower of the Casbah, Above the River Draa

Hush, and be here, and
hold me like a cobra.
I'd gladly lie this way a few more
centuries, my fingers
knotted in your mane,
your pelvis twitching still in aftercome.
For the stars nailed our bodies
together with silver pins:
think of the lucid blitz our bodies made!
Now the sweat on your breastbone breathes like pine-resin,
the smell from your lap is white flowers.
And this will be the way we lie forever—
two lazy gods, gone rampant
here at the top of the world.

Beneath us, the desert says nothing.
No presence stirs. The shadows come green.
But arching above the night, the sand and the burnished craters,
your panting traces birdwings in the sky.

Morocco, 1941
Dennis Lee

Same Place, Next Night

Your slender body is at rest
and the moon, coming to a crest
begins to play chess on your chest
with the lacework of the battlements.
I tried to be your inner guest
but stopped at your skin's perimeter
and now I shamefully confess
that I was still much the happier
of the two of us. We part at dawn,
I'll watch you till I'm able
to see the night's spider who spins
a star over your navel.

Morocco, 1941
George Jonas

Tense Night

1.

Oh horrors, I am splitting apart.
Did you do this to me?

Half of me has embraced you,
automatically, my love.

Half of me is staring at you,
with a cold eye, my statue.
My mind is recording these impressions
seismographically.

This latter activity is involuntary,
believe me, but premeditated.
And now I am lying here,
telling you all about it.

Pleasure was once brought to us willingly,
as if by one raised in servitude.
We summoned that person to our throne,
a slave before a pair of tyrants.

He reeled drunkenly, he panted,
his eyes were wild with light, his steps quick.
We knew his pleasures well. They cannot be taken from us
by violins or fate, by misfortune or sickness.

It is a wonderful thing, this certainty of pleasure,
this insolent and victorious confidence in each other.
Now side by side, we pant,
though our bodies are scandalously quiet.

I embrace you, whose belly is as cold as a snake,
whose hipbones are as sharp as twin knives.
I embrace your waist in our moist memory.

All around us, beneath tables, in corners,
there are earnest genii who care for us.
Your feet, protruding like the neck of a giraffe,
nibble away at the shadows as you stretch.

The moon moves about the courtyard's
checkerboard, russet in the dusk.
It is playing chess. A breeze goes and comes
with the joyous scent of our love-making.

2.

What is there to say in the silence?
I looked for you until I found you.

There were many puzzles to solve, many labyrinths,
but I found a way out of all of them.

I could have searched for you among the light years
of outer space, but I would have missed you

out where hundreds of shattered planets spin,
out beyond the great spiral nebulae of Orion.

Or I could have lept like a grasshopper
into lunar craters and asked: Are you there?

And beyond the Pleiades I could be sifting
nothingness and still I would not find you.

And I could have set foot on earth in the era
of atomic power and mechanical men,

or in the past when Caesar flourished, or when the Koran
was embellished, but I would miss you, too early or too late.

And I could chase after you today without success
on the shores of the Niger or in distant Asia

but I would turn into an age-old, tired-out, broken-down pilgrim
before I could find you among three billion people.

Our meeting is as impossible as if somebody
dead a hundred years had sat down between us.

Smoke from dead fires, aromas of last year's dinners
can be apprehended easier than you.

It is easier for the pin I threw into the ocean
to be found than that I find you.

Time and space and endless indifference
stand between us. This pleasure is taking hold of me,

now I can kick a hole in the wall of our house
because, despite all the odds, I have found you.

Mauritania, 1941

Before Dawn

Under your cool clavicle
your shadows are blue.
Five o'clock says my watch.
Your ribs are fences,
I pass along their slats,
an enchanted traveller.

On my wrist my watch says five,
the crescent of your hip
declines to my horizon's end.
It shimmers, frosted like ice.

My watch glows five a.m.
Your elongated legs, my love,
are roads that are white
through the morning mist.
They meet, not only at infinity.

Morocco, 1941

Desert of Stone

Before the rising of the sun
we drank our goat's milk, chewed our dates,
and were underway to make the day's distance,
under the hanging walls of barren rock,
between the towers of rubble,
that make up this Michelangelo-esque
panorama. Nothing moved but us,
not a cloud was above us.
Like transparent bacilli, red sand swam before our eyes.
Like this passed our caravan,
followed by nothing but murderous sunshine,
sterile loneliness,
soft breezes, silences, stones.
And like this passed the forenoon,
like this passed the afternoon,
as if we had witnessed the world before the creation of man,
or after his final extinction.

Morocco, 1941

The Desert

The line of tents across the crest of the hill,
when I turn around to look back at it,
resembles the spine of a sleeping woman,
to a departing lover who steals a glance at dawn.

The desert looms. You taste it with trepidation,
neither trees nor grass, neither smoke nor water.
It resembles an immense room without walls,
a stage across which nobody dragged scenery.

There are no balconies, no audiences to applaud,
no interludes, no draperies to hang above your head.
There are two curved shapes here, earth and sky,
and you to stand between them, you and your monologue.

Search out a place between the shadows of the rocks,
to sit and bury your head in your hands,
until your thoughts become audacious adventurers
and deep pleasures instead of boring routines.

It does not take long. The mind bores through everything.
This is no world of sentiments and whims.
Up and down exist, there is nothing sideways.
Right and left are no more than a Fata Morgana.

Raise your fishing net. Throw back the small fry,
but when the big ones flash back and forth,
lower it for the great questions, haul them in,
throw them around yourself, ask these questions:

"Grains of sand trickle down an enormous hourglass,
through its narrow neck of glass we flow too,
into nothingness, and when we are all run down,
who will turn this rundown clock rightside up?

"Where is the creator, and what is it he does?

Does he play hide and seek, here and there,
smirking all the while because we will never catch him
in the traps of our mind and human experience?

"Or is endless space void, a solution formed
of the airy custard of nebulae, the milky way,
the red tails of comets? Is mankind nothing more
than a rare skin disease on a single planet?

"And is pleasure the small change that nature
drops into the laps of our parents,
to beget new slaves, who work and who suffer,
and when almost dead are sold into nothingness?

"When our life is like the last ditch of death,
when for a pleasure someone suffers all life long
why do we kill time, why do we make children,
is pleasure really such a great pleasure?

"Will we not be judged by this age in which
we live up to our necks in cities of concrete,
working hard, without pleasure, will we not be
summed up in such a way by a better posterity:

"Their path was a false one, and as their path
so their lives, an ocean of blood and torture.
We ripped their histories from our textbooks
and began everything all over again."

Rattle your toy high in the sky, O child,
not you, old man, riddled with doubt,
for the evening has descended and its hand
is caressing the white nape of your neck.

Nor can you escape your kismet,
nor is there knowledge beyond the limits of knowing.
Now do you understand why this is called the Quarter of Solitude?
Out of this desert come savage men on horseback
and gods on foot with staves in their hands.

Khorb el-Ethel, 1941

Satyr by a Seashore

He sleeps in the abandoned pillbox by the sea's edge.
His skin is like a wild chestnut's.
His lean boyish beauty is heavenly.
All he has is his knife and his whistle
and his tattered white burnoose.
No one even knows his name.

With the approach of dusk, women come to him
with bread, cheese, meat, water
and tobacco. The first one crawls
through the opening in the wall. Cold concrete
serves for a bed. The evening breeze pants,
as do the five waiting women.

In the morning he bathes in the sea. In the afternoon
he wanders the hills and dales.
Then he searches out pre-pubescent girls,
and among the bushes he impales one
and then another with his ease,
like a child pinning butterflies to the wall.

Morocco, 1941

On The Tower of L'Aisha, in the Valley of The Draa

Like a pillow of air, my sheer delight
raises me up and nearly makes me pass
out. Embers glow in my mouth. My teeth are tight.
Under your bronze skin your bones smell of brass,
in a tepid sky the full moon is white.
Your arm cradles your head on a mat of grass.
Perhaps you're sleeping now. Your breathing's light.
Not me. I stare at the cheeks of your ass
that swim like swans in the mercury lake of night.

Morocco, 1941
George Jonas

The Casbah

The new moon's curved scimitar slices
the sky's reddish-purple pot-belly.
The Haroun al-Rashid of the evening's shadows
has begun to distribute his disguises.

The casbah is waking up. Over streets and squares
and alleyways, the dusk is honey-like and heavy.
Smoke materializes outside an opium den,
extending its insubstantial hand to be kissed.

An obese pasha crosses the room to the bar,
a green corpse whose eyes are as dull as tin.
Over there, a British physician. He feasts
on smells and feels well. Across the stage

moves a belly dancer. Her navel is a well
without walls. Into its thicket of shadows
a soldier, absent without official leave, peers,
panting, dying for a trickle of water.

From the marketplace come drum-music and torch-smoke.
The moon armours the sword-swallower's breast.
Around the storyteller a silent crowd fathers,
the lips of all are open: Sinbad returned home.

A Tuareg squats, his back to the high wall,
he stares at the spectacle for forty days.
Suddenly all of this: drums, daggers, veils,
eyes of women behind the veils, the bazaar,

copper plates, smell of mint, palm-trees,
deep green shadows and flat white walls,
circle and dance before your eyes until you too,
caught up in it, spellbound, hear it cry out:

"Your country is in ruins, your wife an old nag,

your work contemptible, your life an agony;
come, disappear into these deep dark alleyways,
where life is sexual and death pleasurable.

"No law or order exists in this quivering swamp,
no news or letters from home can reach you here:
Disappear, die and resurrect in a hundred forms,
there is reincarnation even for those over thirty.

"Strip off your clothes and your past in the Moorish bath,
drop your morals to your ankles (so much nonsense),
forget your name (you were bored with it anyway),
and drop your memories on your wrinkled underwear.

"Hang your notions on the nails (they are nothing
but rags unloaded by greedy merchants),
do not once turn round, be happy once again,
young and as naked as your mother bore you.

"Be a smuggler, a thief, a pimp, a fishmonger,
prefer boys to girls (believe me, it makes no difference),
be a robber or a murderer, and mortally embrace
the walled quarter of this city built on rock.

"Or are you bored by the city and enthralled
by a more exciting end? Seize what it is you want:
stretched out on the purple hammock of opium,
astride the green saddle of the horse of absinthe.

"Or remain here, do not move, glance about you,
listen to the songs of birds that never existed,
until the constellations wheel about your forehead
and rattle in the wind like slowly ripening dates.

Tangier, 1941

The Final Night

The sky is unfathomable tonight and has the keen smell of copper.
Everything moves, vibrates, circles about: nervous twinkling lights,
galaxies, crystal nebulae, planets, even stars beyond stars.
Never before have I witnessed such a wonderful display of fireworks.

My right hand lies under your neck; and I am lying flat on my back.
Our hipbones are as white as milk and they touch together.
In between your hipbones lies your belly's crater, filling with
        silky sand.

What is on your mind? The same as on mine? The thought that,

Once separated like this, we will assume over obligatory posture
for all eternity? Above us the sky and a furlough of earth,
below us our broken spines and thighbones, two worm-eaten crutches
cast away, unneeded now. Among our teeth passes an ant and a rush
        of water.

Between the ellipses of your hipbones there is a central hole
        through which
fell your intestines and sex. But it will still be good.
Your china-wear flesh cracked apart. Yet like the white wing
        of an enormous
butterfly, it will lie there, at attention, as if awaiting love.

Should I cry out that such things cannot be? I would rather hold
your hand and mutter my thankfulness to What I Do Not Know:
who pulled me out from nothingness, who patched my body together,
        piece by piece,
who placed before my eyes this indescribable lens with which to view
        our world,
who put me down beside you and permitted me the possibility
        of loving you.

Do not mourn, do not tremble, do not rage against death! You will
        curse in vain.

Life, like lust, is a short cramp, then nothing. We will be covered
with brown or yellow earth. And about our hipbones, like a piece of
     clockwork,
the zodiac will continue to circle about us as do our loincloths.

Morocco, 1941

Weeds and Foolscap

1. *Glassblowers' Lane*

The molten glass revolves:
gleaming, multi-coloured spirals.
The bearded old man puffs into it
and we smile. But smiles are fleeting,
we should huddle together and weep,
for we are shattered wine glasses
and there is no glassblower
to melt us together again.

2. *Nettles and Poison Ivy*

Nettles and poison ivy flower in Christ's footsteps,
the Prophet's Book is but a thicket of lice,
Persian teachings are children's tales,
and the Hebrews are lettered but ignorant.
The hospitals of this world have two wings,
one for the fools who believe,
one for the fools who disbelieve.

3. *Banana Peel on the Street*

Banana peel on the street.
Its silken side is smoothly alluring in the dust,
like the *derrières*
of lithe and elegant ladies.

4. *The Doughnut-Maker*

Fat dark Moor. Looks down from on high,
from his doughnut barrel,
along the length of the street. He would smile
if he could. Children
approach him for doughnuts,
the young run, the older walk.
But to him all the walks of life

are the same. He exists,
a swirl of purplish smoke.
For him there is no street,
his seven arms folded,
Buddha-like.

5. *Still Life*

Yellow apple on a white plate,
leafless, stemless,
like the rear-end of an infant
awaiting its enema.

6. *Typhoid Epidemic*

The hospital: curses perch on its roof.
Arab women approach; over their shoulders
hang little boys like withered vines.
The physicians — nine youthful doctors —
play chess with death, night and day.
Now and then, one may manage a draw.

7. *Colony*

Apoplexy saves herself for French customs officers,
the French disease sweeps across the sky like a meathook,
sailors' balls come clunking down like so many rotten walnuts,
Scorpio sniffs at the surveyors' private parts,
jaundice spots the governor and licks his lips,
undulent fever rattles the foreign bankers,
mosquitos on high are on the lookout for the Foreign Legion,
all six districts sprout poisonous mushrooms,
pesilence flowers like a novel fungus.
All this constitutes our inner line of defence.

Morocco, 1940-41

Brothel-Going

Tommy speaks:

The wind's whistling through our hair.
What a gorgeous Sunday afternoon!
The car engine makes such sweet music.
There, on the left, is Mark Twain Park,
and that's the Great Snake River
(it isn't as bad as it sounds).
And here we are at Newburg, Missouri,
where seventy-seven houris await us!
(*Listen to the racket from the cat house!*
They'd doing the tango in the dark—
whoever likes his gin warm
will shed tears to get back in.)

The whore:

Come on in, sweet soldier boys!
Why so surprised?
What are you gawking at,
haven't you seen a she-ass before?
What's your Division? Seventy-fifth?
Where's the tall kid from?
Boston, Duluth, Peoria?
I can tell this one's a Frenchie.
(*So my ass flops over the chair?*
That means I'm bubbling over with good health!
So I can heave my busy tits over my shoulders?
Look at the fun you're going to have!
Any God-damned nigger'll die before he gets me!
White, black — gin, sin!)

Come on, heroes, it's getting late,
let's go up to my room and have a talk.
My lap's a treasure, deep as a cave,

my thighs are white as chalk,
their treasure and pleasure await you,
Tom Sawyer! Huckleberry Finn!

My answer:

When we learned, but were too young,
quite early one morning in school,
that love is a monster that rides
upon mares and chickens and sparrows,
we grew pale-white and swore an oath,
in the courtyard of that school,
that we wouldn't be part of any such thing,
certainly not as long as we lived.

No, no, so we prefer to walk away,
to climb up some hill or other,
return to the barracks, shed our clothes,
make love to the pillow.

We prefer basketball, or sprinting,
and thus sweat out of our desires.
I prefer to pitch my cap in the air,
play my shoelaces like an accordion,
stare thoughtfully at the evening waters,
or fasten a dead rat to a string and twirl it about.

Newburg, Missouri, 1943

Aurora Borealis

The heights and the depths appear as they do from an airplane:
snowy clouds or snowy landscape, up and down the same.
Frost sits over everything and does not step aside for spring;
it squats with its green darning needle knitting the Bering Sea.

We landed. For seven whole days we hunted the Japanese.
I shared my rations with the seals on the shore.
I gave up rebelling against everything. All I see are Eskimos
and the top hat they added to the crown of their totem pole.

Beneath the hanging carpet of the fog, buttoned into fur,
my body buried in snow like some machine-gun,
I exist from day to day. You are not even a memory.
Yesterday you came to mind when it was getting dark.

In the kitchen the cook muttered something about the Aurora
	Borealis.
I stepped outside the door. The lights shimmered over the ice fields.
They were wonderful, bluish and fading away in the distance.
And they reminded me of something from the distant past.

What did they remind me of, I wondered? In serpentine motions,
light and shadow played, shifted, and turned away. Doorknob
		in hand,
I stared at the lights in amazement. From inside a sharp voice
		cried out:
"Close the god-damned door!" I remembered; they reminded me
	of your skirt.

Kodiak, Alaska, 1943

68

Darwin's Rubber Plant

"Soon we will reach the Tree of Darwin."
The Polynesians are trying to cheer me up.
But I am so enchanted with
the blue peacock's tail of rippling sea,
so enchanted and so angry
that I do not listen to them and hear
only the cooing in my eardrums
of the pigeons, wild, half-mad.
What angers me is the thought
that I have come here too late—
too late for marriage, too late for sex—
that I was summoned
for a hurried shedding of clothing
at some dry and frustrating orgy
by the exhibitionism
of this rude and naked landscape.

"Here is the rubber plant. Five hundred years old.
Not a branch has died.
A long time ago it was visited
by Ferdinand Magellan and Charlie Darwin."
And it grows here: a piece of left-over scenery
from the last day of creation.
It flashes back the sunlight
with the ten thousand mirrors of its green leaves,
this rubber plant, this enormous
elder brother of volcanos and prophets.
I was squinting, however,
draped in the flowers
of this luxuriant garden,
at the serene slopes of the bay
where the blue of the water appears
sprinkled with yellow-coloured dots,
as if someone had rubbed

a blue and yellow iris
between his fingers. "So,"
I said insolently to one of my guides,
pointing accusingly at the rubber tree,
"it never flowers. A rubber tree
without any flowers?"

"Of course it has flowers," the guide answered,
parting the leaves and yanking out
a spear-shaped sprout, a rigid bloody twin-berry.
He held it aloft like a knacker the scotum of an animal.
"That's not the fruit of the rubber tree, silly,
that's its flower." "Take it, please,"
he said, forcing it into my hand,
but I refused. "It's not very interesting."
"It is," he replied, pulling it apart.
"It has two sections, see?
One is the stamen, the other the pistil;
between the two is this hard shell-wall,"
and he held it before my eyes with pride.

"I see it," I said, uneasily.
"How does the pollen get from
the one chamber to the other?"
"That question everybody asks.
The shell-wall has pinprick-like holes,
and an invisible parasite,
tinier than a pinprick,
eats the pollen and carries it
on its little body as it crawls through the tunnel,
just as the miller eats bread
while carrying a sack of flour on his shoulder.
"Understand?" he asks, with a triumphant smile.
He throws the fruit of the berry away
with an obscenely quick movement,
and leaves me alone with the rubber plant.

Humbly I bend down and pick up
the flower of the rubber tree,

and touching its shell-wall with my fingertips,
I wonder what Charles Darwin had to say about this.
How did he fit it into the Generation of the Species?
In the churning of the plant's uterus,
how does the parasite find
the flower of the rubber plant?
How are they able to exist
for so many years one without each other,
why does one of them not starve to death
or the other remain forever barren?
And the tunnels through the shell-wall,
how did they get there?

Did the parasites bore these holes?
Or were they there first,
specially made for the parasites?
How is it parasites are able to discover
and apply the necessary geometry?
Or does the rubber plant's cells
know instinctively what the parasite
measures in micromillimetres?
Or, one evening after creation,
did an entire regiment of parasites
march out of all the rubber plants,
in double columns, stand at attention
and listen while the captain of the parasites
gave orders, telling them what to do next?

This is what I sit and wonder about,
there is no law and order,
it is all senseless and insane,
this play and its production.
Lifting the fruit up before my eyes,
I suddenly experience an enormous joy,
for I can now peer into and through the little holes
— telescopes lined with purple —
and see a hundred shades of colour
dancing in the sunshine, kaleidoscopically.

"I understand him now, the master of peeps,
of parasites, and of men, who sculpts
the stars and the specks,
so lonely and cruelly,
who disappears into the telescope,
filament-like in the little vein,
and emerges again at the other end.
That is whom I did not find
when I searched him out
in New York, in Vienna, in Budapest,
he the heavenly director
who summoned me to a secret rendezvous,
here, in Samoa,
secretly and so late,
too late for anything
but a hurried shedding of clothing,
so that he could show me,
just once, his naked being,
he the director of the fireworks,
so that I would have this occasion
to applaud him,
he who gives birth to all,
the impressario of everything,
who then casts aside what he will not have,
the fireworks, the planets, and me.

Pago-Pago, 1944

A Pilot is Speaking

What are you bothering me for? I don't like talking,
you'll only wear out your tongue with all those words.
Want a cigarette? Drinking I like, and going to the movies,
so I can get away from myself for a while.
Why are we fighting this war? What a dumb question.
Did you dream it up, or did Roosevelt tell you to ask me?
Why would anyone want to know what we're dying for?
You think about it — when you're alone, not now.

Damn it all, I've offended you. Look,
I was a lanky young man, full of good will
(Seventh Airforce Station at Saipan,
Jim Oleson, write it down if you need the details,
twenty-five years old, an engineer, Baptist,
Army Serial Number 0 165 132 50,
height 6'2", unmarried, a Major,
born Hartford, Connecticut) who
would drive his car a hundred miles an hour,
would whistle at the girls, never bought a newspaper,
would raid the refrigerator every evening,
would stand for hours on end at the bar. . . .

I volunteered, there was nothing to keep me at home,
and then this tremendous feeling overcomes a man . . .
this oceanic feeling — how can I explain it? —
when I take a dive and suddenly the air pressure
pitches the plane back, or when I fly blind with radar in a fog,
or when I hitch on my automatic pilot
and lazily survey the horizon for a while,
or when the anti-aircraft guns give off puffs of smoke
like miraculous smoke-rings,
or if one nose-dives straight down to the earth
and the plane is rocked by an explosion,
a second and then one sees nothing except the blue sky
and to the left there peacefully stands Fujiyama.

Preparing for our twentieth mission against Tokyo,
before dawn our dog bayed outside our tent,
blue rings appeared around our eyes,
and I knew our number was up,
the Japanese Emperor was sneezing blood that day,
as we approached it the Ginza was already crumbling in flames,
we dropped everything we had, and in a crazy mood
I made a farewell circle above the city,
we flew away leaving everything by the seashore in smoke,
the docks, the ships, all the buildings, large and small,
then I glanced backwards at my buddies
and I saw we were leaving behind a trail of blue smoke.

I was all alone in a rubber dingy
(the others swimming around me should have been buried),
and I was pleased to be dying alone,
my first moments by myself in three years.
Then a flying fish landed near me,
I grabbed at it and shredded it with my broken fingernails.
The seventh night I drank sea water
and started to vomit blood. I knew it was the end.
And I remember thinking,
as I pitched backwards in the dingy:
Thirty years from now, even right now,
what difference will it all make. . . ?
And then I heard very softly the songs
of pilots who had crashed over the Empire.

Military Hospital, Atlantic City, 1945

French Intellectuals, 1946

Look at these men of pale and intent faces,
hear these women of no secular graces,
in this land they live and prosper like weeds after a rain.
They earn their living by singing the praises
of Russia where they'd only earn a bullet in the brain.

Paris, 1946
George Jonas

Poet's Return

St. Socrates, where are you now?

Eight years ago, during the days of oppressive feudalism,
the lord of the castle, though he knew me not,
wrote me a letter and invited my wife and myself
to his castle. He wrote because he had never known a poet,
and we accepted because we had never slept in a castle.
He was old and wealthy and unmarried, with two Rolls-Royces,
in one of which was a bed with a chamber-pot,
chinawear from Sèvres. Beneath the chandeliers,
within walls of watered-silk we dined, the three of us.
The wine stewart brought us three bottles of French champagne,
we usually consumed one, the balance being thrown out the window
onto the patio because nothing ever went back to the cellar.
Occasionally guests would arrive, counts, barons, air force
officers, cavalry officers, but never an infantry captain.
In the gloom of the garden one evening, I sat on a bench
beside a general who said: "I am a Communist, too,
my boy." "But I am not," I retorted mildly.
Our host had an enormous library, behind glass and mahogany,
two thousand volumes of penny dreadfuls, bound in calf.
We accompanied him on the tour of his estate. By the gate
his peasants doffed their hats and scraped the dust.
Although invited the whole summer, we could take it
but a week. The gallant old gentleman, our host,
pinched my wife's bottom for the third time,
so I phoned my friend, a Social Democratic deputy,
in the neighbouring town. Guests were standing around
when his cab entered the gate and pulled up before the castle.
We thanked our host for his hospitality and got into the cab,
while the noble guests loitered about under the portico,
glaring with hatred at the rotten plebians who were leaving.

Eight years later I returned. From the neighbouring town,

through the mayor of the city, I got a guide, a very stupid one,
It seems two years previously his lordship had taken refuge
in his Rolls-Royce. By the gate, a howitzer knocked his head off.
Nobody was certain whether a Russian or a German did it.
Now I walk through the great salons. The watered-silk
has been shredded by Russian bayonets. All the windows
are shattered and working their way in are wild vines,
so we are walking in a green semi-darkness. All the furniture
has burned for cooking. The chandeliers are on the floor.
Every evening, my guide explains, couples come here
to make love. I look around. In the corners there are heaps
of straw, used condoms, and round plotches of turd.
"After doing it, they shit in their beds, the pigs," he said.
From the suffocating semi-darkness we go into the garden,
and I sit on the bench in a garden gone to seed.
The guide stands beside me. I would like to send him away
so I could hear myself think, but I do not do it.
I see the garden wall is riddled with bullet holes,
the height of a man's head, and heaped at my feet
in the green grass are vicious green cartridges.
"Were there executions here?" I ask. He shrugs.
I press forward. "Who killed whom? The SS,
Russian prisoners of war? Hungarian Nazis, Jews?
Hungarian police, Communists? Communists, police?
Russians, Hungarian soldiers?" He does not answer.
"Were you around during the war?" "Yes," he replies.
"And you don't remember?" "I've forgotten all about it."
"Or is it you don't intend to remember?" For a time
he is silent, then he looks at me reproachfully:
"Tell me, please, Mr. Faludy, does it make any difference?"

I turn away from him and stare at the grey bullet holes
in the whitewashed walls. St. Socrates, where are you now?

Hungary, 1946

At The Funeral of a Byzantine-Like Party Theoretician

A detachment of plainclothesmen hides among the bushes
and twenty uniformed policemen form a line with tommy guns
defending — what could it be? — this funereal mound of earth
    and the police state.

Cordons come in two kinds: the inner and the outer.
The inner one contains Muskovites, party bosses, journalists,
foreign ministers who murmur among themselves
    — showing the flag — the carcass is but the pretext.

The outer cordon contains the spontaneous masses so forcibly
transported on trucks to the tomb of the great deceased,
among whom an agent weaves in and out, noting the names
    of those too busy to come.

The great deceased! For twenty years he resided in Moscow,
this alone was enough to make him great and famous;
in passing, he sat through five Party Congresses,
    surviving all five, this phenomenon!

He had such a firm grip on the Party line,
all they had to do was slap him sharply on the ass
and he would engage in self-criticism, thus becoming
    a true philosopher.

They dubbed him a philosopher. The Party granted him
this position when he diluted the texts of Stalin and Lenin
and quoted them either-which-way so as to meet
    the prescription of the day.

Besides, he was a hypocrite, ruthless, cowardly.
He would kick whoever was lying on the floor.
But as far as the assigned asses were concerned,
    not one was left unlicked.

What was really on his mind? No one ever knew.

He had no friends. This was how he remained faithful
to himself and to his Party. Alas:
     our age, man and his world.

An orator arises to give — one would assume —
his account of the deceased, but it is not to be so.
He explains the ins and the outs of a week of politics,
     that Truman is a turd,

That in its fight against the effete sages of the West
the party holds its banner high and here,
on this ground, while he lived and worked, stood
     the deceased philosopher.

The orator concludes. The assembled multitude feels
the nervous need to applaud — the aching urge is there —
but we disperse. We learned our two lessons: to applaud,
     to step upon one another.

I remain standing near the Kossuth Memorial,
my heart beating well up into my throat.
Unless I outlive these bandits, this is how
     they will bury me.

Do not abandon me, my friends, leap atop my mound,
maintain that there was something human about me,
that I would eat my brussels sprouts with butter,
     my corn-on-the-cob with black pepper!

That I was wont to speak in Arabic in my dreams,
that I was both stupid and well-educated;
but do not abandon me to my dejection, friends,
     Wesselényi and Gyula Illyés.

When you have interred me and then dispersed
to the nearest café, there begin to speak about me,
spontaneously, without knowing fully why,
     to midnight and after,

and should an expression, or a shade, be missing —
for the life of you no one can understand why —

then my life has not been like this Byzantine sage's,
  utterly in vain.

Budapest, 1950

Ode to Stalin on His Seventieth Birthday

Genie, out of the sea, wrath of deep waters!
who spits mud and whirlpools into the sky,
you would bottle up the future of us all,
then heave the bottle back into the sea.

Your brow, portal of the new Middle Ages,
your armies, at attention, by its gates:
there is none among them not your lackey by birth,
none that has a thought even from hearsay.

Your scientists: fools, people paralyzed,
dangling from spider's webs, scratching in the dust;
your economists: tarting up the only-born
son of your system, eternal misery.

Your writers: an honour guard of flatterers;
your friends: one division of slavish fossils;
your poets, by a mixture of mud and blood,
limn the background of your golden Byzantinism.

You Titan: born of an unhappy marriage
of fatal powers — malevolence and intelligence —
the turnkey of nations who, singlehanded,
strangled an entire revolution.

Its heroes, you had them strung up
or shot in the back of the neck — but not before
spitting in their faces and directing
your dirty boots into their staring eyes.

Scaling the mountain of corpses, ever higher
— with solemnity yet joviality —
you survey the enormous marsh of your empire,
horrible hoodoos, boundless powers.

Your terrible apparition, glowing of sulphur,
towers over the puddle of this century,
for you are more gigantic than Genghis,
audacious than Attila, treacherous than Tamberlaine.

So wildly do I yearn for your death,
I try to conjure it up — I nearly go mad —
I spy on you, as you pace up and down,
in your study, in the Kremlin, alone.

Suddenly you keel over — a stroke —
taking your table and chair down with you.
A hive of guards, with sour-cream complexions,
buzzes in the flies about: "Look, he's dead."

Or I visualize your liver with its cancers.
Where your veins and arteries meet, cancerous growths thrive.
"Wait, wait," I say, "one more minute, they will gobble you up,
there is no medicine in the world to help you now."

And I have this dream that I have become invisible
and I race — ships and trains speed me along —
and I catch up with you in the darkness of your bedroom
and tear out your throat.

Millions would do the same. I want nothing
out of life but your death. O you curse of the earth,
who built your Byzantium out of dried clots of blood,
O you, Byzantine monster, Constantine the Great.

Budapest, 1949

To Suzanne, from Prison

> *There is no greater pain*
> *Than to recall one's happy times*
> *In misery. . . .*
>
> (Dante's *Inferno,* V)

I trace the gallows in the whitewashed prison-walls,
for sixty-six days now I have not seen the sky,
but pain and sorrow, past and future, interest me
half as much as they did when I was with you.
Only now do I realize what a giant you are,
neither fear nor death can conquer you in me,
so I materialize you here while I walk back and forth
among the half-blind gnats flying at my face,
and I tell myself this poem, from which I feel
the rhythm and the rush of our love,
while I turn over in my mouth, like the sweet kernel
of an apricot, your sweet name, Suzanne.

What Dante wrote about lost happiness
nobody can understand as well as we.
How many pleasures we left untried
on the half-laid table of our love!
Now you are alone. Persecuted because of me.
I feel your tortures incessantly.
Do you still love me and do you ever think
of our child, the one we never had?
I see him often! There is a sparkle of gold
in his eyes. And his hand is as soft as moss.
It will be too late, will it not, when I return,
as pale as a soldier assumed to be dead?

Before I return home, I wonder how many months
or years? One, two? Whatever happens, wait for me,
wrap those memories around your waist,
memory's flag, like a virginal banner!
What we saw and shared should bind us together,

and grass, trees, sunshine chase away everybody else,
the abandoned lifeboat of our conversation
which the algae gently rock with their green hair,
the taste of strawberries in your kisses,
our travels to lakes and forests,
the shapes we assume in our sleep,
like a womb, or a tomb from the bronze age.

And if it is ten or twenty years? I will endure it:
my eyes will retreat in their sockets like train lamps
you see at crossings streaming by the fields at night.
My flesh will dangle from my bones like dough,
my semen will be lifeless, unlike the wheat
from the pyramids that survives a thousand years,
but limping or crawling in the mud, with spreading cancer,
still will I arrive to have a look at you,
so I might sit once more beside you on a bench
in summer, your silver hair among the shafts of sunlight,
and then the horror of this vision here
will be as sweet as an ocean full of honey.

And if I have to die, with one foot in the grave,
I will still profess your everlasting faithfulness.
Evenings in autumn, on the soft sandals of falling leaves,
I will send you the sound of my steps passing by.
I will immerse myself in frosted glass and fogs,
but the dawn and the deepening water will show me up.
When you are dozing in a chair, I will come upon you
like a bird flying blind through a fog.
And from the storeroom of dead noises, my voice
will accompany you on all the roads you travel,
like an invisible stream will flow alongside you
through cellars and among the roots of trees.

Do not choose a husband who listlessly
or nonchalantly holds you in his arms:
you must feel desire when you cry out and remember me,
the soft Orpheus who has gone:
with whom you try to play hide and seek but in vain,

yet I will find you even in the night:
or when you go boating alone to watch the clouds,
in cavernous cellars or in the shade of the pergola,
I will look at you from the dark hue of wine bottles,
in the gleam of each and every grape I will be there,
in the waters I will float by with a broken neck,
in the shapes of clouds I will make insolent faces at you;

I come between the two of you in bed and board,
I toast with my glass the heavy wine of memory,
which grows clearer and sweeter as time goes on:
so you will feel ashamed of your husband's bald head,
and thus you will hate his hacking cough,
and his ankles which are beginning to turn tin-grey,
and at nights, when you are both old and wide awake,
I will take my stand at the far corner of your bed and glow;
then you can cry and gasp for breath among your pillows.
You live in vain and where is your victory?
Me, the old carcass down in the burial pit,
I will be victorious and beautiful and youthful for you.

So shall our love triumph, this is what I sing,
dead lover and desperate prisoner,
this poem, a sweet violin at our late marriage,
or an organ heard beyond the grave.
This is hard country. Do we tumble together or apart
over these precipitous years?
What I send, an arrow going farther than myself,
is that this poem should be long-lasting!
In one hundred years it will make no difference whether
we were paid here with pleasure or a plot of earth,
but down the echoing corridors of time,
I have tried to shout out this poem of mine.

Cellar of the Secret Police, Budapest, 1950

85

Western Australia

For two days a postage stamp circled in the air before my eyes.
I saw it for the first time in my childhood, it was an early issue,
and it depicted a great black swan, the navigator of mild waters,
and along the bottom it said, in stiff letters, "Western Australia."

Australia a century ago, even now it is taking shape before my eyes,
a train of covered wagons cutting through the mud, oxen yoked
    together,
and bearded menfolk marching alongside, energetically, jerkily,
shaking their fists and waving about their great long-stemmed pipes.

Silver light cuts across the clearings like an axe.
On the shore of the lake, complete, so peaceful, stands the cottage,
the smoke from its chimney spiralling upwards, chain of an anchor
from the depths of the sea spiralling upwards to the fleet of the stars.

Women hurry by in purple taffeta. About the mounds of their breasts,
revolve children like the spokes of wheels. The womenfolk
peer into the depths of great mirrors, edged in heavy metal,
where they appear so pale, but they never seem to age at all.

Few newspapers get through, and when they do the news is always late.
They hardly know what Bismarck is up to, who bungled at Khartoum.
But inevitably the first smooth pale road is blazed through,
and then, in buttoned jacket and yellowish beard, the telegrapher.

Irish stew cooks on the kitchen stove all evening long,
and the ever-more-plentiful sheep return like the sirroco,
from Adelaide they bring the miracle of batteries for the flashlight,
the little boy's water pistol, and his mother's fur muff.

Rarely does the family dine together — days of rest are privileges —
but in the smoky inn, the kerosene lamp dangling from its chain,
they give expression to the sentimentality that overtakes them,
and they drink kegs of beer to the health of old Queen Victoria.

Time is measured by grandchildren on a garden fence,
by autumn winds across the crystal face of a lake.
Christmas comes with the heavy thump of plum puddings,
and ripe apples fall in unison from the thick-leaved trees.

I stop abruptly, I have been caught *inflagrante,*
and I feel ashamed of myself. My two years in prison,
my dark cell, a few slaps, and the fear I feel are enough
to make me run away in pursuit of the beautiful black swan.

That I, still an awareness in the mind of a people,
might forget my calling, my country, my fidelity and fame,
that in my dreams I might work free of an alien stake
and emigrate to another continent, a new pioneer,

and become, too, the subject of the dead Victoria,
I, not a living slave but a serene corpse
that yearns for little more than the feel upon my brow
of your glory, your own free-flowing earth.

Not like this, I insist, and I feel a wild smile
sneak across my features, and I declaim without a word
that I will never desert my flag or my people,
that I will ever fight, though the fight be won by others.

A hundred times will I begin anew, a hundred times in vain,
until you become like my father's house, my fatherland,
though one day I am sure I will visit Australia
where I hope to catch and bring home that happy swan.

Recsk Prison, Hungary, 1952

Monologue on Life and Death

As one insane with love loves
to roam avenues covered in autumn leaves
with streaming hair under the tumbled sky
so did I love to roam over this earth.
Or as a traveller in unfamiliar towns
explores the streets on his first evening there
running, gaping, trying to look his fill,
and feels enchanted, in a happy daze,
that he has found the city of his dreams
where all is new: the display windows' gleam,
the colour of the drinks in the cafe,
the passers-by, dressed as if for a feast,
the wild thyme smell of genuine liberty,
and yearns to stay for ever and a day,
as he does feel, so felt I for this world.

I knew: here all is new and never would return,
a rare, supreme, fleeting phenomenon.
Butterfly soared, I said: "Look at it well,
you see it now, but then never again."
When drinking with a friend I showered him
with love and words as if at dawn I'd die,
for I always did fear that at the break of day
there'd be no friend, no wine and no awakening.
Others fear so, but lock it in their brain.
However I, I wore it on my brow.
From deep within its prompting pit my mind
never ceased threatening: nothing endures.
This tiny spark between non-beings's clamps,
this miracle of being that I am,
a bright glow-worm held in doom's toothless gums,
the ever-present, chilling consciousness
of evanescence: these gave my life its taste,
colour, delight, magic and infinite glory.

These made me frantic and inspired, and
conjured up for my eyes fairy-tale visions
from the wasteland of mere existence.

Intoxicated with the tart wine of earth
I flung my arms round concepts, men and things
as drunks embrace the lamp-post in the street.
Thus did my world become a work of art,
the starry sky a Gobelin tapestry and
three-dimensional space a warehouse filled with
bales of experience where the watch-face turned
into a laden table for a dozen guests and
my seconds dripped away like heavy honey drops.
This is how I became the lover of the earth,
the great idolater, Romeo of the clouds,
the troubador singing beneath towns of the dead,
carver in rhymes of gothic cranellations,
the naked priest of pagan midnight swims,
until the sands ran out and I, transient phenomenon,
vanished in the timeless sea of transient phenomena.

Recsk Prison, Hungary, 1952
Kathleen Szasz

The Execution of Imre Nagy

He made his inventory at dawn,
pacing under the vault of his cell;
everything was in order,
only his prince-nez was missing.
Another minute had passed. His conscience was clear,
and in less than an hour his stubby legs
would catch up with Lajos Kossuth, Rákóczi, Dózsa.

What gave him his claim?
Was it apathy, courage, character?
Or did he know that halfway there
he had solved the riddle of the century?
And what made him great and beautiful?
His faith? His intentions? His honesty?
The end? Force of circumstances? I don't know.

Maléter was coughing
in the next cell. Suddenly a cold draft
touched his forehead. Should he ask for
paper and ink? What for?
What for, he thought. Papers drift away
like leaves in a storm,
and among them walks serenely, with measured steps,
a stocky gray-haired man: the deed.

The end. He guessed it would be hard
but by now it made no difference
—the door opened: cursing,
the goons jumped on him with iron bars,
crushed his shoulders
and broke his arms
and then they placed a leather strap
under his chin and tied it around his head
so that standing under the gallows

he wouldn't be able to say *Magyarország,*
and they kicked him along the corridor
and he stumbled, half-blind
without his *pince-nez,* then pityingly
he looked around the courtyard
but couldn't make out the hangman's
frightened face, nor Kádár
who stood there cowering, drunk,
flanked by two Russian officers.

Then there was only the lime, butter-soft,
spreading over him like a billowing
toga. Soon it began to sink,
took his shape,
fastened on him and petrified.
It dissolved his skin, his flesh, his face,
but it preserved hair by hair the friendly curl
of his mustache, like the nation.

Since then the days are skinny
hollow-chested seamstresses
and the nights are sweating whores,
though sometimes when I'm half asleep
a gleam of light falls into my eye—
it might be distant lightning
or a playful searchlight
or the lamps from the next street,
but it could be his *pince-nez.*

London, 1958
Stephen Vizinczey

East and West

To J.R.C.

In this country I speak freely, without fear;
but no one in this lethargy will ever hear.

Back *there,* all listen to what I have to say;
especially the secret police, who lead me away.

London, 1962
Eric Johnson

White Mice

They are so awfully fecund, the poor things,
you must do something, love—
my wife informed me,
so I rose like someone under orders
to carry out an execution . . .
someone who is afraid because he knows
he too is composed of dust.

My goodness, with what frolicing
was I greeted by the mice!
Their noses at each other's backs,
they tobogganed down the steep little ladder,
and how they beat each other up,
and how they played with one another,
the lewd little things!
I imagined I was seeing ancient Rome,
Sodom, and Nineveh.

I picked up and shook the cage,
directing the mice into the toilet bowl,
and pulled the chain
so they would be carried away
quickly by the "Niagara" action.
But no, the foaming whirlpool
was not strong enough to suck them down,
so the mice clung to their lives
with greater intensity
than the rush of the water.

They shot by as pale horses
that leap steeples in a race,
like greyhounds or grasshoppers or flying fish.
Gripping the chain,
I yanked at it again, but no use.
No water came and I stared
at the nightmarish splashing.
I stood there petrified until the mad

swimming pool had calmed down
and their weak feet reappeared
elongated in the water's mirror.

I would have run away
when I spied there, crouched
on the seat of the toilet,
a slimy miserable specimen of a mouse.
With its red eye filled with thankfulness
it looked me in the face,
perched there, shivering like a sailor
fresh from a shipwreck.
In its wet happiness it seemed to be praying
to the lord of the mice,
who grants him his daily bread,
who builds him his spacious cage,
who . . . against whom, when he almost
drowns him in the water,
he harbours no resentment.

But with its new and pink paws,
so cramped it stuck to the seat,
so filled with love,
it looked me in the face, straight in the eyes,
that I turned away to stare at the wall
and then I closed both eyes
until I slowly convinced myself
there was indeed a mouse but only in my imagination.
And suddenly I felt I was growing,
like someone possessed of a divine power,
with all the necessary dignity and cruelty.
And so I stretched and grew taller,
simultaneously I shrivelled and grew shorter,
during which I realized I could not be a murderer
without being a victim as well,
and at long last, with closed eyes, I began
to see myself in the place of the little mouse.

My knees gave way. Nauseated,
I crossed the kitchen floor
and went outside into the wet garden.
I reached out and held onto an apple tree,
but before me the little red eye of the mouse
circled around me,
and then I vomited all over my clothes,
me, the god of the mice.

London, 1962

Love Poems to Her, Dying

1.

I escort Eva through the roses; she's
with Andrew, who will spend the summer away.
You — standing by the window, white as death —
with your slow left hand feebly wave goodbye.
Then you turn round. The car soon disappears.
Do you know you won't see him before you die?

I think of how not to betray myself,
and cross the garden, creeping like a snail.
Seated in the chair, the corners of your lips
drawn tight, plumb my eyes like a well.
Is it politeness, is it duty, or
unfailing love that binds me to you still?

This lasts a minute and soon you are calm.
"Talk about yourself," you say dryly: "In
these things it is you who are my debtor."
And I talk. Before long you discover
what I am thinking about. And of this
we could moan endlessly to each other.

The two of us are seated facing death
and staring at the summer sunset.
The boy is gone. And a child is a child:
cold and without pity.
He will hate you for leaving him behind
and me for having stayed.

London, 1963
Andrew Faludy

2.

Each morning you are more sallow, more tired.
As I comb out your hair I find it breaks off.
Your arm has dried up like a vine. On your neck
lumps of cancer are swelling. Through the window
the sky is blue, the mountain slopes indifferent.

Today you feel no pain. I sit beside you
on the bed and hold your coffee cup. In place
of little breasts are purplish pustules.
I have this dream that you will not go away,
that we will remain together one decade more.

My love, my sceptre, who weighs eighty pounds!
What is there to say? Blessed be this day,
for the spirit still flickers in your ravaged body,
for your eyes, pastel-grey, are still beautiful,
and even like this life is marvellous, never better.

Soprabolzano, 1963

3.

You've dozed off.
In the moonlight from the window
your chin is all bones and angles, like a corpse's.
I take your wrist again, and
again I try hypnotism:
"Don't die! Keep living. Want it because I want it!"
I've whispered the words a thousand times by now;
I whisper them again.
And as I repeat the spell
my eyes slide over your wasted frame once more, with the cruel
superiority of the living over the dead.

You used to think the soul was an
overnight guest in the body
one day it would simply
depart, making its way in the new dimension.

But I was afraid that soul and body die together,
step by step,
the way you're dying now.
And nothing helps: not
X-rays, not spells, not love nor
medication — till
here you lie, adrift on a narrow bed,
a small boat going under.
I hold a tattered rope, pathetic arm.
It slides from my hand.

Soprabolzano, August, 1963
Dennis Lee

4.

Five thousand years ago I'd have brought a rope
to tie up your body, sweetheart,
to prevent your ghost from returning.
Today I wish: if only it *would* come back.

A thousand years ago, relatives would have sat
like demons in the corners. A wavering candle-wick would burn
and we'd await the instant when your soul
would make its exit and soar into the sky.

Today it is assumed that all we leave behind is a carcass,
more dead animal for the garbage heap.
But five senses don't suffice to grasp
the entirety of things. This is my only hope.

Soprabolzano, August, 1963
Dennis Lee

5.

The roads of day and night
become black and white striped snakes.

You ask me why I stay with you

who can offer nothing now but horror.
Don't I loathe your strangled cough,
your back violated with bed-sores,
the blood, the moans, the sweat?
Why must I remain to watch you die?
And, you hiss, what can *I* do to help?
Do I want you for another ten or twenty years
pouncing upon me every night
like a vampire, a succubus, a vulture?

There are enough strangers to nurse you.
And don't I know how vain you are
when I'm around? And that you aren't afraid
of death, and will find the way without my help?
"Get out!" you gasp. I should go down from the mountains
to Verona and care for you no more.
I must forget you, simply conjure you up
as when once I saw you in prison:
harmony, beauty, light,
an astral body hovering above me;
then I should go on to Florence
and after taking rooms in the Via Salutati
proceed to offer mundane daisies
to Hora in Botticelli's Primavera
whose eyes and lips are so like yours.

And when you've sauntered through matter
to the immaterial and gotten used to it there,
it might occur to you to visit me,
on a whim, on a moonless night:
I'll never know for sure if I've embraced
your comet-blue nebula of a body.
But because you loved me, you who
died so young, you will be merciful
and leave on my belly
the silver residue of lust.

Soprabolzano, September, 1963
Gwendolyn MacEwen

On Those Occasions You Walk Towards Me

On those occasions you walk towards me on the sidewalk,
it is always nightfall, and I always tingle with pleasure
when I realize that you have found a new body for yourself,
and that once again you are as slender and as girlish

as when we first met. Then I walk all the faster
until an uncharacteristic step or an indifferent smile
betrays you, for you make me wince the way you take cover
within the bodies of other women, the way you assume new roles,

the way you flit back and forth all night long and flick pictures
off walls whenever I sleep alone, and whenever I do not
you gently breathe down the nape of my neck and sputter

along with the wood in the fireplace, you rash and untamed angel,
and I rejoice that you still enjoy playing with me,
although I know that I do no more than play with myself.

Florence, 1965

Lorenzo de'Medici, about 1480

A pool for fishes they dug at Careggi,
at the zoo's edge, an immense one,
as he had ordained it. Alas, they lacked
the proper knowledge. Fishes of each kind,
mammals and amphibious creatures too,
were thrown in, whatever they could
procure from Arab, Venetian, Portuguese
and Turkish seafarers.
                            Before dawn one morning,
he rose as usual before the birds.
The Medici entered into his sleeping garden,
and at his pool halted. The water was dark
yet transparent. A column of crimson,
the crimson robe of the Prince.
A fish was spawning there, hoving
near the shore. Beyond it another fish,
purple, thin, a cannibal, bid its time,
then consumed the eggs as they streamed out.
A catfish, with the moustache and the sly,
lewd look of Emperor Frederick the Third,
sucked out of the mud butter-yellow worms,
as if it were eating macaroni. Farther on,
knives of silver darted about and clashed.
A goldfish — whose tail was not there — became
a crescent moon in the rigid polyp's embrace.
A skein of white intestine near the shore
rocked in the valleys of the waves.
On the floor of the pool a peaceful snail
advanced.
                    Approached Master Ficino
from the villa beyond the dark cypress trees
(who had lost the sleep of an entire night
pondering a single sentence of Plato's).

Quote he: "Master Lorenzo, My Lord,
what can be the matter? You seem pale
and so silent. Are you not well?"
And Lorenzo replied: "My Ficino,
until this moment I thought I was God."

Florence, 1965

The Poet Abu Nuwas to Haroun Al-Rashid, 790 A.D.

With knees drawn to my chin, like a grasshopper,
I lie in my cell on an iron rail.
Remember me, great Caliph, do not suffer
your servant Abu Nuwas to perish in jail.

Forgive my transgressions. The holy law,
the Koran has become my only joy.
I hold it as I used to hold, with awe,
the silken backside of a growing boy.

Tanger, 1964
George Jonas

Sonnets

1.

I swing, strung from your shoulders:
in your deep eyes I suicide.
I drop my defences and on my knees
I surrender with a kleenex.

I strip off more than clothes.
I expose myself: bare-naked,
mother-naked. My only defence
is my delicious lack of defence.

I again renounce my friends, even my son,
the way I did when first we met.
That meeting! Let me lick your ankle.

Let me grovel. Like a teenager,
let me grope at your toes and grow up:
ah, my forehead is circled with stars!

Malta, 1966

2.

Like a cobalt shadow at your ankles, space grew.
And in the universe: nothing. Nothing but you.
The clock stops. Beyond your shoulder
The palm trees explode, and are not true.

At the window, performance of the light-ballet,
Your face engages passage of today,
Jasmine from your shoulder names the month.
Our neighbours are beyond the Milky Way.

Furniture, like weightless trapezes and empty tents,
Float and flap between us. When I turn:
Dust is falling on five continents.

Then nothing but the torque of your presence in the room,
Below: loquacious calm of the sea,
Above: pirouettes and pirouettes of the moon.

Malta, 1966
J. Michael Yates

3.

Where does your body leave off?
Where does your being take over? Beloved,
I never get it straight for even your
toenails are totems to me, your kneecap is
godhead.

Sweet holy meat. You're on the stairway, coming
down say, and what am I fixed by? Your
feet, they wake cadenzas in the spirit. And also I worship
the burning bush in your groin . . .

What more can I confess?
My body's in jail, thank God in
you and my whole being stretches out to its horizon, you:

whom I do love.
Flex me, flex me, I can't pant any harder.
In my heart you are being torn apart by a leopard and a dove.

Malta, 1966
Dennis Lee

4.

Starved lion of my passion, savage beast of prey
padding this jungle on its four soft feet
hot for your love. Now my lips on their way
to yours graze your throat. Days and nights never meet

while I explore you. Your body looms between,
barrier to love. Oh it's plain you're not there

105

when we touch. But you sleep in vain. Behind your screen
of secret burning flesh I track you down unaware.

Raw bitch, for you I'll neither pray nor wish evil,
my pact with your soul makes me out the Devil;
why care for your cheap nakedness, the lean

melons of your buttocks, freckled shoulders? Rather say
that I turn from you to find you, somehow mean
in closing my eyes to see you better elsewhere.

Malta, 1966
Raymond Souster

5.

Your face in dream becomes the dawn, and down
to the dark breath of your sleep I, vampire, lean
to breathe you like a vapour that gives me life again
and of your flesh I eat, your blood, your brain.

Love, in your hot throat my aching head is lost,
O kill me or complete me! Or take at least
this stark corpse in your claws, this beast,
and love him, for you and God know his needs best.

But I think I have killed you — or have you killed me?
Crushed and torn the last of my fears apart
so I might waken dead each day on your dark breath

with seven blades of blissful sin stuck fast in me,
with the swords of all sweet joys and evils in my heart
and blood on my mouth from a kiss as red as death.

London, 1967
Gwendolyn MacEwen

6.

From the corners of your eyes youth send
plum-blue flickers of pain toward me.
If I had any honour at all
I'd stay away from your sweet mouth.

Perhaps even now it's not too late
for me to shake off your hang-dog loyalty and throw you out.
Poor lunatic, what do you expect
from me, a poet, in a room between cracked walls?

Is it my face you love, puckered with poverty?
Wake up and look ahead.
All I can leave you here is horror
when the worn puppet tumbles down.

Take your hand from my yellow hand
where the water of time is trickling out.

London, 1967
R.G. Everson

7(a).

High above Central Park, every cloud
gives birth to yet another jet.
Why was philosophy born so early
and scrapped so soon by technology triumphant?

Why not vice-versa? Why didn't Archimedes
forge cannons and atom bombs fall
as Nero sang and Rome burned? Then the past
would be a crumbling monster,

a warehouse of ugly machines, and the present
a crystal dawn. We could talk of virtue
without anyone making fun of us

and how happy we'd be! The mind
of man would float like an eagle in the clouds
while Socrates was making his *début* on Broadway.

New York, 1968
Andrew Faludy

7(b).
Children are playing in the dust of Central Park,
licking their ice-cream cones and staring at the sky.
So I ask you, Why the past, why the future? Why were not
the engineers and the managerial élite here before us?

Why has not Alexander the Great flown to the moon,
like some aerialist? Why has not Julius Caesar
turned out tanks on a long assembly line, and why
has not Nero dropped atomic bombs upon our heads?

Over complacent ruins, on wings of wonderful crystal,
rises the eternal drawn. In flowing robes of blue,
our lips almost parched, we would stroll about and discuss

the meaning of life and, oh, how we would titter.
Reason we would see eagle-like glide across the sky,
and Socrates would appear crossing Broadway.

New York, 1968

In the Reading Room of the British Museum

Sitting next to me is a middle-aged woman who wears
a drab housecoat. She has on shabby tennis shoes
(it's winter) and her brown woollen stockings
are fastened by strings around her calves.
When she goes for a smoke she opens a cigarette tin
and takes out a butt. I strain to see what she is reading:
it is a large-size codex in cuneiform writing.

At quarter to nine each morning, I stand
by the columns and wait for the doors to open.
The regulars are standing too, or arriving on foot
from their bed-sitters in the neighbourhood
where they cook their meals and live on God-knows-what . . .
the woman in the drab housecoat, the young man
who fell in love with a poor mistress, Egyptology,
the old fellow with the ruddy complexion who studied
the universals and their problems for half a century.
Gradually I make the acquaintance of all of them.

It shames me a little to be among them
because they do not scribble notes the way I do.
They are not being paid by a university, an institution,
a publisher (how little mine pays me for my work),
but that is my fault. I have come from a country
where their kind are no longer even tolerated.
A dying people for whom every day is a holiday.
Only on Sundays do they sit, somewhat forlorn,
conjuring up and about them dead civilizations,
resurrecting them because ours is dead too.
Rather than machines, cars, money, there is something
they have that I, like a medieval monk, can believe in.

Unknown gods have been their hosts on this earth,
and when they stiffen in bed for the last time,
they will know that their lives have had a meaning,
that they have not lived vainly, as have billions of others.

London, 1967
John Robert Colombo
with Eric Johnson

Northern Summer

A bird as red as a poppy (I don't know its name)
chirps good-mornings from the tree's branch.
I walk by to bathe in the bluish brook
which flows into a lake that remains nameless.
In yellow sunshine glint sharp blades of grass,
swords from the Bronze Age for self-defence.
In the distance are clusters of raspberry bushes,
Christmas trees with red bulbs of frosted glass.
Beyond lie boulders with glacial planes.
I am sorry I came too late to this region
to find my writing desk out here. Virulent
verdant moss smothers the brownest boulders:
the last time I saw such angry green stains
was across stagnant tributaries of the Amazon.
For several brief weeks, the sky, the sun,
the day, the flora, play tropics here.
Buds rip apart with the speed of torn silk.
I love that red flower with the hairy stem
which has four leaves and resembles a thick
blood-clot. (I don't know its name, either.)
Creepers work their way along like watersnakes,
and where the brook forms a little pool,
waterspiders race by in some competition.
Yellow and blue butterflies chase each other,
dragonflies float by upon each others' backs.
Everything hurries, blooms, grows, loves,
Pollen-scents, flares, splash in the air
like tiny things aware their ends are near.
I run, as well, to the nameless lake,
and alongside me, young, transparent, silvery,
panting, with bunches of flowers in her hand,
races the summer season, my mad Ophelia.

North of Magnetawan, 1968
John Robert Colombo with Eric Johnson

Ave Luna, Morituri Te Salutant

To George Kaali Nagy

1. *In praise of the moon*

Mere moon, I would not notice you,
I'd only bay at you, mere light,
but you are coloured green and smell of lilacs
and you are coloured amber, fat and bloated,
and translucid and bloodshot
and you are more than mere moon,
not just a light, a signal
not just a sign, a symbol
not just a view, a vista,
a disk at dusk, a discus,
companion on my brief
journey to nowhere, like the trees,
mists, grasses, fingernails.

I nearly touched you as a child
with my hands, fetish of mystery,
a bright coin carelessly dropped
you rolled under the skirts of clouds,
you sprinkled flour on Grandfather's mill
the cemetery and the cows
a distant millstone in the sky.

Full moon, my young years' semaphore,
I celebrated you with the firewheels
of sound, simile and metaphor,
Ophelia's mad breast floating naked
in the dark waters of the sky,
a clock-face cut of marble
in hopeless love with untouchable time
dropping its useless hands,
a transcendental angel's rump
sitting tranquil
on heaven's latrine
Hercules' adolescent scrotum
as his mother applies the powder-puff

before his virgin rendezvous.

Giant spider, you caught for me in your web
Cornwall, the Ile-de-France, the hills
of Transylvania and Tuscany,
on seashores, meadows, balconies and rooftops,
in parks and boats, upon the copper-plated
battlements of Amar's
tower in the desert of Morocco
over the crowded camel-humps
of sand dunes:
you played your game of chess against my naked
lovers' bodies — I only watched you play —
and if you bent too close their open thighs
they butted you aside, for I had taught them
to play with you, silver balloon of love.

Aboard battleships, at Saipan, Tarawa,
you'd always aim a merciless
searchlight straight in my eye: I'd run or stand
in total darkness next to black trickles
of springs shot dead and fountains still alive
my chest
bedecked with your medals of mercury;
and how you shone after the war
over Fifth Avenue and Budapest
round, well-fed silver carp
I watched you floating
sprinkling your roe along the Milky Way
and I began to hope,
under your sign the beerhall of the sky
still welcomed guests of every constellation
each in his favourite place
to regularly meet night after night
though many chairs stood empty at my table.

Seven times seven bars, double barbed wire,
and two more lines of barbed wire beyond
the window of the punishment cell at Recsk.
Past the wire only the bluefox firtrees,

shadows of death—
I stepped into the rigid tinfoil
of your cold rays and quietly thought
a transmission belt
a Jacob's ladder
parallel rails running with me
to the white terminal
of eternity—
but Stalin died and left me all alone.

I wouldn't mind seeing you still today
the same as forty years ago
climbing up slowly, red-beard dwarf,
along some gnarled trunks of oaks,
or make you once again a tangerine,
balloon, ideal cheese, shaving mirror
that absconded with a foamy face,
but I shall not complain—
you did follow me faithfully
to Vienna, London, Malta
and once more across the sea
while staying fairly put at home;
only last November in New Jersey
at Andy Hamza's house
full of music, books and symposia
stepping outside the glass doors
I drew quick breaths of pleasure seeing you
on the asphalt-hued branches of the sky:
silver apple in my winter garden,
frozen apple in my winter garden.

By that time I knew that they would reach you
or rather that they would reach your namesake
the satellite, the planet circling
around us, three hundred eighty-four thousand
kilometres away, the objective moon
which, as other bodies, contains its functions
and occupies a space in space

and equals only its own self, the moon
that's only so much and no more, no legend,
anxiety, toy, magic or hypnosis,
godhead, memory and all your other faces,
the real moon, that revolves in distant skies,
of which I'm no part as I am of yours
who are in me and would not exist outside—
so they will reach the moon,
I thought, and I was glad
that they would reach it in my lifetime
and I could keep you still for comfort
and sacrament under the black
cupola of the night and of my old age
and even in the brutal crypt of space
for my death candle.

2. *The conquest of the moon*

Eureka, shouted Archimedes
in the bathtub and a single jump
took him into the streets of Syracuse
to proclaim from the rooftops the news
that the apparent loss of weight, et cetera;
"Land, land!" yelled the lookout
from the masthead at two in the morning:
Mary, mother of God, he was right after all,
the captain, this loud-mouthed, greasy faced,
slavedriving fake-Italian
sham-Christian kike;
he will not have to walk the plank at dawn,
we've reached the treasured shores of India!
And only sixty years ago a crease
in the clouds: Wilbur Wright entering Paris!
Along the Bois, in gardens, parks,
a biplane on every strip of grass,
dressed in straw hats and checkered pants
eternal adolescents would
tinker at night: I can still

smell their carbide-lamps and the blood,
airframes made of rulers, walking-sticks,
bedspreads lifted from hotels
or their aunts' old skirts the wings,
and how did their engines spit and sneeze
and what savage cries would rise
to heaven, when one of their grotesque
grasshoppers cleared a bush or two!
Then came the trees, later the hills,
the Channel, the Alps, the sea, the ocean.

"Moon, moon!" I thought before the picture tube
waiting for the great act
(no small time stuff, Columbus, Blériot)
listening to a commentator who
was demonstrating on a full-scale model
how when and where would Armstrong and Aldrin
emerge from the module and how many yards
would they walk after having cleared the ladder
take photographs put lunar soil in sacks
exchange a few words with president Nixon
raise a flag after the lapse of a certain time
by what process would they re-enter the spacecraft
how many pounds of ballast would they leave
behind how many seismographs — and as the broadcast
was not on schedule, he began to talk
about early utopias of space
mixing Aristarchos up with Lucian, Samos
with Samosata, pronouncing Cyrano
as Kyrano, and telling us finally
that we may celebrate
for in this historic moment
mankind has entered the lunar age.

He repeated all this three more times
when the desert-like moonscape
appeared in a black sky
with the Eagle's contours like an old stove

standing in a museum of science,
then the transparent phantom
of Armstrong's abdomen, then Aldrin
as they tiptoed, then walked and photographed
according to plan, faultless and precise
performing as predicted, as if a bizarre
exercise in gymnastics
wearing barbarous masks, while the younger
generation grew restless watching the screen,
lit cigarettes, giggled: these two
have been shuffling their feet for half an hour
and still there's nothing, not a single shot
has been fired, a dragging production,
so it's been done, we've seen it, is that all?
Man lands on moon is technology triumphant,
boredom supreme.

But I stayed on with the older
people in front of the set: kept yawning,
and hoping that perhaps this once
after Hitler and Stalin
after Rotterdam, Belgrade, Oradour, Coventry,
Katyn, Auschwitz, Warsaw, Dresden
after Nikita Khruschev, Lyndon Johnson
after Budapest, Dallas, Memphis, Chicago
and Prague
there will be something
to be happy about
something to celebrate,
and from our houses
where the bird-claws of terror
keep scratching at the windowpanes,
from our insane, endless main streets,
our superb eight-lane expressways
where we can drive ourselves at sixty miles an hour
into misery,
from our boldly designed concrete bridges
that connect our garbage heaps,

from our lovely landscapes hidden
behind billboards advertising them,
from our forests wearing plastic rags,
our mountaintops wrapped in waxpaper,
and from our ocean
whose billions of hollow whitecap-teeth
fail to chew up not only the shit
from our oiltankers and factories
but even our old-fashioned and useless
rubber safes—
from everywhere
we might look at the moon and lick
our chops: we've screwed you too,
we've made you sweetheart just in time before
our rotting bed has collapsed under us.

Is there
something for me to celebrate?
The two daring astronauts
and Collins who is now circling above them
will be celebrated well when they return
to earth; and if they're wise enough
to retire, even in thirty years'
time they will have plenty on which to live
golden letters will list
their names in history books
and golden letters have a sheen of gold
assuming of course that in thirty years
there will still be books and history.

Hurrah for the crew, by all means!
But is there a captain,
who is the Aristarchos here,
the Columbus, the Wright, the Blériot?
Hail, then, the creators
of rockets, including the pioneers,
the designers of V-2,
hosanna to all

who had tied rocket-wings
unto the ankles of thermonuclear
bombs to make them fly
from country to country
from planet to planet,
hosanna to all
who in the concrete bunkers of reactors
breed from the very excrement
of science
purple toadstools of destruction,
who manufacture and deliver freely
the hot spices of mustard gas to dress
our last bowls of salad who recommend
our stone-age instincts white
phials of anthrax for a sedative,
who handed our chicken-brained leaders
the pushbutton of remote-control death
for something to play with,
and who, because the speed of our madness
is still far, far behind
the speedy wonders of technology,
equipped our asses with Niagaras
of solid-fuel propulsion,
hosanna to all
they celebrate along with us this evening
or rather permit us to celebrate them
modestly, as becomes mechanics
who do not work for glory

but for salaries and bonuses
paid out of public funds
who discreetly leave off
the word "military" before their titles
and whose lives
are guarded by plainclothes police, better
than my life or my cleaning lady's life
should we walk across Central Park at night —
they celebrate along with us this evening

except they know, this is no opening night
or even dress rehearsal, it is a bold leap
into the void; the rest is an attraction
for the clapping crowd, a circus act,
featuring the three astronauts
as the clowns of outer space.

The live coverage is over —
the newscasters explain
how Armstrong, Aldrin and Collins
will go in isolation once they're back
on earth for twenty days, in case
they picked up germs,
while our scientists will analyze
the lunar soil because they half expect
to solve the secrets of the universe
locked in these rocks — then some new commentators
praise the event by using the word Peace
as frequently as Cortez used to use
the name of Jesus Christ — do not believe them,
each sentence is a lie:
the ad-men of technocracy are cheating
they're lying, these chief engineers of death,
they know full well it is not on the moon
that there are germs; it is inside their heads
that both culture and science have become
a culture of germs,
they piss on the universe's secret
unless there is a government to buy it,
they piss on the rock samples of the moon
(whose Chief of Staff will spend money on rocks?)
they look for something else:
the bottom of a precipice or crater
on the lunar Sea of Tranquility
where they can put
a missile base, much more splendid than any
in Hitler's or Stalin's fondest dreams;
they will equip it fully in a few months

and aim it at one half of the earth,
then in a year or two some jaundiced,
lead-lipped and perspiring
Party leader
with the aid of a Lenin Prize or two
and a few bullets in the brain
will force a Soviet spacecraft into being
and a missile base in the Sea of Storms
aimed at the other half of the earth
and at us in the moon,
and from the moon we'll aim at them
on the moon
and from the earth we'll aim at them
on the moon
as we have aimed at each other on earth
mutually for some time,
and then we'll start all over once again
the game of the atomic bomb, new nations
land on the moon —
                    Enough!
the profile of von Braun comes on the screen
at a press conference, he's carefully
averting his eyes, perhaps he's afraid
his eyes will give away, but what is left
of him to give away?
He utters measured words, his jaw-line strong,
a classic nose, pure pleasure on his lips:
this man will never notice the dark
cape of werewolves around his own shoulders —
we have degenerated into instruments

in their hands helplessly; to swallow strychnine
may be a consolation but no defence against them,
nevertheless: no murderers have bored me
half so abysmally as they do,
these incarnations of the counter-human,
the schizophrenic gorilla
the cosmic gorilla

the suicidal gorilla
who has come to execute
the judgment of predestination
who is spilling on us
nature's ripe wine of fury
who shakes
our monstrous kind off the rim of the earth
whose patience has long been exhausted —
listen to Caesar, for he is victory
but he does not mean whatever he tells us
and he won't tell us whatever he means
he did conquer the moon
but did he notice her colour, her smell?
Listen to him no more
kick his loathsome television to pieces
his lunar lunacy
as the last act of a heritage of freedom
walk out into the garden, taste the trees
drink up the grass, run your fingers through
the moon's quicksilver hair.

Toronto, Summer, 1969
George Jonas

Letter to the Mayor of Philadelphia

Mr. Mayor, the undersigned,
George Faludy by name, a poet
by profession, a teacher of letters
at Columbia University, having found
the cost of living in New York too high
for his mean salary, in October last
came to settle as others before him
in your community of brotherly love.

Further,
having left behind quite a few milestones
on the thruway of his life but still
not being tired of it, he did
in good faith and on his friends' advice
equip his front door with the required
steel locks & chains, and he did renounce
much against his desire the nightly walks
regarded previously vital for his soul
and sinews, and he did
observe the local custom of squatting
in his own apartment after sunset
in the manner of his cave-dwelling, fur-pelted
ancestors, listening to the shrill
sirens of squad cars passing in the dark
much as they did to the trumpets of mastodons.

Note, however,
that even so he couldn't avoid his fate.
Last Friday
under blue skies, broad daylight, after lunch,
on his way home from the library
he was set upon around the corner
of a street known as Cyprus by some kids
—luckily only three, and not much older
than fifteen years of age, still clumsy
and inexperienced black bachelors
of crime —

his fellow pedestrians
pretending not to notice the event
passed him by with their necks pulled into their collars,
whereupon he did with dispatch
take the sizeable screwdriver from his shirt,
his only support in the jungle, which you,
Mr. Mayor, insist on calling
a metropolis, and with this instrument
did strike the mandible of one
assailant, who spit out some blood
and two of his lower teeth, and quickly ran
after his friends. George Faludy
picked up his books and walked home. He drank
two pots of tea to calm his nerves, then called
the police, who came, took notes, and shrugged
their shoulders. After which
he began to prepare his own notes for his lectures.

Mr. Mayor, the undersigned
can almost hear your answer: "Sir,
you are bragging and not complaining.
What else do you want? You have suffered no hurt
or damages. Take my advice,
and if you have to go out call a cab."
He, however, having given the matter some thought
has reached a different conclusion. As soon
as possible, he will pack his belongings
and return to Canada, where he does not yet

have to be confined to his quarters, to Canada
which has still not been so completely ruined
by the hailstones of prosperity and progress.

But he is as ready to give advice
as you are, Mr. Mayor. Kindly leave your car
at City Hall one day and venture forth
for a few hundred yards along your city's main street
any time of the day, and stand
at a corner, perhaps just long enough

to acquaint your nostrils with the smell of blood;
or do the same at dusk, taking a side —
street if you are bold enough, until you note
the furtive way the passers-by will size
you and each other up, then risk a closer look
at the alert bulge of their hidden fists
as they sneak and slide past one another
or dash out of their own front yards, or take
cover behind their doors — please view them
until you feel you have fallen among
a mad houseful of raving lunatics
and then you might realize that you,
the mayor of this city, are in fact no mayor,
and (much worse) this city is no city any more
for here the inhabitants are bound no longer
by any common purpose, faith,
emotion, principle or interest,
the social contract has been torn up, its pieces
flushed down the sewers, and the statue
of William Penn two hundred feet in the air
now only serves as an elaborate scarecrow —
and, further, you might realize that this is still
not all that bad, because it will be worse
tomorrow, not to mention next summer,
until in ten years' time the babies
will scream for heroin in their nurseries,
the pallid breath of smokestacks, car-fumes, riots
will hang still in your air, not to be swept away
even by tornadoes; your police
will guard in tanks the houses of the rich
and leave the rest to fend for themselves, while you, sir,
will refer to the seventies in a public speech
as an idyllic era, a golden age,
where humans had the innocence of doves,
with a nostalgic smile playing on your lips.

The undersigned
can offer no solution. Neither can you,

Mr. Mayor, for presumably you would
if you could. But if you can't, stop drawing
a salary you don't deserve. For once
be a man, face squarely your function
and position on this earth and take
the consequences. Your suicide
would help no one; besides your ancestors
used to regard it as a sin, unlike
the keeping of slaves. Your resignation
would make no difference. Consider instead,
the towns of Alexander, Constantine, Romulus,
were held together not by bricks and stones
but people. When the people
have lost the power of community
no reinforced concrete and no computers
can hold together Philadelphia.
Call, therefore, on the City Council, sir,
and have them resolve that whereas (one) legal,
hygenic, ethical, historical,
humanitarian, but most of all
practical reasons, they abolish hereby
the Corporation of Philadelphia,
and whereas (two) the population may
regard the city non-existent from this date
and should, within a certain limited time,
take freely to the hills.

To serve as an example to your people
be the first to take a carpenter's axe
and cut your car to pieces (the internal
combustion engine has become our curse
along with the nuclear bomb) and buy
a covered wagon, some oxen, horses
(it may surprise you to get
ten head of cattle for the price of a few steaks)
take your family and head east, beyond Medford,
in New Jersey, no one lives on the land,
construct yourself a modest home, then play

with your grandchildren under a green arbour,
and forbid them
ever to build cities.

Postscript: the writer
sees no more chance than you that his
wise words may still be heeded. But if
by some miracle you personally heed them,
here is one more suggestion: of all rubbish
that science heaped on us in five centuries
take maybe one: medicine. Then watch from a distance
as we are buried under the rest.

Philadelphia, February 23, 1970
George Jonas

Apocalytpica

To George Jonas

The future has claws, and they hold plutonium.
There is wine in every glass and it all tastes sour.
Each man I meet is filled
with a fury to change the world,
or his God, or his sex, or his cuff-links, but never himself.

For thousands of years, our lives had a single motion:
back and forth on the plains of destitution.
But now we dance hot-foot
on a mountain of gold-plated shit.
And every Mini Minor is steered by an Alexander the Great.

We're riding the crest of the wave, in the age of effluence.
Don't call it unclean if you value your own health.
The neon gleams like dawn
to the average senseless man,
and the band plays on, and the ship goes implacably down.

And Justice is impaled.
And Beauty does a fade.
Technocrats and politicians,
Party hacks and profiteers,
Bosses, managers, and every
Murderous man in the street:
I hail your insatiable gut.
Because of you we shall never again regard
The mystical root of the Good.

New Jersey, 1971
Dennis Lee

On My Father

How you were afraid for me, of people,
of myself. How softly
you beseeched me: Don't turn into a cricket,
nobody listens to crickets these days.
Your good advice ran off me
like water off a duck's back—
the only person I could follow was myself,
so I became what I am today,
that in my old age I might chirp,
cricket-like, in my own inveterate,
incurable happiness, Old Man.

Are you indignant? Your tombstone,
white as a beggar's hand,
reaches up for me:
it begs remembrance.
So be it! Come among the glowing embers
of the fire we shared, insubstantial ether,
reveal your frayed being,
the last time before eternity.
Your son, a conjurer from way back, invokes you,
your son, the insolent lout, summons you up.

Appear, so I may sketch your portrait
faithfully, my soft-fleshed,
full-chested, short-legged
Dad, a deep-sounding cello—
the chrysanthemums of your hair
tremble on the nape of your neck—
better than Einstein's, your strong neck—
I remember you standing here,
between your two Bunsen burners,
on the verandah of the past.
Come nearer, throw yesterday's pride
to the winds, and let us come to terms.

We argued and we quarrelled
in vain, on the verandah,
between your two glass retorts,
in your smudged white smock,
you stood there and warned me:
"Don't become a poet,
nobody reads poetry these days,"
and how you asked me if I realized
what would happen to me
if I settled my hopes on the unsettled,
and sought matter in the immaterial;

with such patience you explained that
blessed science brings peace and prosperity,
and should I become a chemical engineer
I could be sure my bread would
always be buttered, and I could
write the poems I wanted on the side.

I stood there, facing you,
hatred bubbling up inside me.
"No, definitely not,
I need nothing from you,
neither your name nor your advice,
neither your manners nor your way of life,
neither your science's dynamite
nor your pre-Raphaelite furniture,
neither your blessing nor your estate,
nor do I need your beloved German
philosophers from your library,
and the blessed day will arrive
when I will leave this house for good."

Sometimes I would enter into the arguments
but most of the time I would stubbornly bite my tongue.
But even then you would guess
what was going on in my head.
And I would know too what you were thinking
when you would turn away and stare out the window
and realize you had no one to carry on

and that you had lived your life in vain.
Sometimes you would add that we
had fallen far apart but that
you still loved me or that
nature was responsible, that
individuals have permutations and combinations, that
it did not matter because the race lived on.
I would retreat to my room
and stare at myself in the mirror.
No, in no way did I bear a resemblance
to that old fool. I swelled with pride
and flexed my pectoral muscles,
flapping my world-conquering wings.

That was some time ago. Since then
I have doffed the wings and donned instead
the monk's cowl of humility.
Let me wiggle out of the monk's cowl
and all the humility, so here I stand
bare-naked, and I know
that I have come by and through you
and that the ruins you left standing
live only in me
until they collapse once and for all,
and that I ought to pluck out my eyeballs
and slice the nipples from my breasts,
that I ought to go into occupational therapy
so they ᵕan change the way I instinctively hold my head,
the way my palate savours the sensation of orange-trees,
the way my leg muscles respond to an evening's walk,
the way my optic nerves respond to the colour blue.
And I ought to search out the preserves,
the amber-coloured preserves of good spirits,
in the damp larder of my brain
where the jars stand, one amber, one white,
with cold vinegar bottles full of the fear of death.
(How much pure honey, how much wine-vinegar!)
And I ought to be able to empty all of them,

if I were able to empty any of them,
to liberate myself from your
personality and your influence today.

Our arguments made no sense at all.
Neither of us was proved right.
I never conquered the world with my poems,
nor did your glorious science, toadying to us,
ever put us on top of things.
Neither of us passed the test, Father.
Your scientific work has been forgotten,
your library is covered over with dust,
your heavy upholstered furniture
was used for firewood by soldiers,
your villa was confiscated,
your plot in Budapest sprouts weeds,
and I am on the other side of the ocean,
a stubborn cricket who chirps
if not for himself alone then for none at all.

I would gladly speak in a friendlier fashion
were you not so enormously far away,
in the half-buried mineshaft of the past,
and did not a precipice, rather than years,
yawn between us, nor was I the cause,
but your dead father stands nearer you
than you stand nearer me
and to him his father and his father . . .
and on to Mycenae and Babylon.
You would speak across avenues to one another,
we would not even nod to one another,
or to each other, for what is there to say?
On the volcano of the present we stand,
facing death, our backs to the past,
as long as the world lasts — days, how many days?
Do you still remember the verandah?
You assured me there that though the individual dies
the race remains. Because it was like this

in the oldern days, it would always be so:
you believed that generation
would follow generation
and that from hand to hand would pass
houses, libraries,
the sides of hills, pianos,
inn-doors, gospels,
concrete and abstract notions,
from one to another, as in a relay race.
Father, we fell far apart,
for you have always held that the aim and crown
of the universe is man,
that the earth is our crude but lasting hostel,
and therefore is home,
that life makes sense,
and that its rough road is made smooth by that.
You, happy and innocent man,
who died six months before Hiroshima.
How far away you all are from us,
old dead people from whom we do not issue,
you fools, running after rainbows,
bouncing the balls of past, present and future
on your heads like playful dolphins,
who made love to but the beautiful
naked Narcissus of one's own death
in the ultramarine mirrors
of non-existent time.
The salt of the earth has lost its savour.
There are no new pages in our history books.
You, my father, crawl back into your shell of nothingness.
I will not try to awaken you again.
Hold fast to the ground about your grave
for a great explosion is about to come,
and not even your bones will hold together.
So let me sit here and cover
my head with my dirty palms
under these blood-streaked skies.

New Jersey, 1971

Characteristics of G.F.

He was overpolite and clumsy.
He missed many chances to mate.
He was shy with people face to face.
He bowed down too soon, rose up too late.
Yet he had neither fears nor inhibitions
when attacking a Monster State.

Toronto, 1973

Behaviourism

He offered me, the chief of the secret police
(from day to day I could see myself growing thinner),
a bowl of soup to spill the beans on my mates.
But I, although a coward and a sinner,
resisted this "positive reinforcement"
(thanks to a faint post-scientific shiver
of ethics) . . . and thus failed to evolve into
a rat from the traps of Dr. B.F. Skinner.

Toronto, 1973

Fort Book

Also known as The John P. Robarts Research Library

Was there a nobleman in Gaul, around 600 A.D.,
(when grasses grew on graves and Roman roads),
who would not, in daydreams and nightmares,
be overjoyed to inhabit such a fortress himself,
had he the wealth? From such a bastille,
from its embrasures and heavy bastions,
he would aim his arrows and pitch his hot tar
down on everybody below him. Such a castle
would deter equally his enemies and friends.

Inside it is different. First the antechamber
(where did the cloakroom go?). Then the chamber,
which doubles as an amusement park where swift-
moving escalators permit glimpses up girls' skirts.
At the top, a haunted castle, replete with surprises.
When you think you have finally attained the stacks,
you are in the men's room. In any other building
you would smile. But such is this edifice
that smiles freeze across their faces.

A few decades ago I made my peace with the greed,
with the pride, with the spiritual impotence
of our builders. But seated at these long tables,
squirming under flickering fluorescent lights,
one will find no privacy, no chance to contemplate,
no way to loose oneself in this book or that.
Young people go hysterical in these surroundings.
One's toes begin to fidget in one's shoes.
On the nicest girls' faces, muscles tense
and tighten. Even a sweet boy's penis withers up.
The best of books is the bitterest of gall,
and the same coffee, which is palatable down the street,
in this cafeteria stinks instead of steams.

Not everything monumental and millionaire-like
turns into a work of art, as the uncouth assume.
So let me pause and propose that the technician
(for I am unable to consider him an architect)
felt no remorse for having painfully foaled
this lumpish building, so tasteless, so ugly,
so lacking in elegance, harmony and charm.
Let him make a pilgrimage to New York where,
shoeless, he should crawl, on hands and knees,
up the steps of the Forty-second Street Library,
singing penitential Psalms every single step of the way.

But if you maintain he created a work of art,
I maintain we should erect a statue to him here,
in front of his own creation, or better still,
let him stand on its dias, himself his own statue,
holding in one hand his boundless self-conceit,
holding in the other a hand-mirror so that we
may watch him strain to kiss himself upon his own brow.

Toronto, 1973

Chief Censor and Secretary of State for Culture
Han Ju Visits Li Ho to Commission a Poem

The saucy stallions paw the air
With pomp and pearls and pommel-flare,
And beam the message everywhere:
    Let Li Ho make a poem!

The rings are gold, the banners blue,
The pennons dance like view halloo
As on they come in retinue:
    Let Li Ho make a poem!

The gowns that graze the reins above
Are lovelier than mourning doves.
The Censor brings a Censor's love
    And news of my commission!

And now the train is at the door.
And now they knock, and knock once more,
And chargers rear and servants roar:
    Their eyes are all on me!

I watch his halo, how it glows.
I wait to catch his first bon mots.
He even writes in rhyming prose,
    This genius from Chiang!

And neighbours say, behind their hands,
That God the Father botched His plans—
But Secretary-Censor Han
    Knew how to make corrections!

And now — he speaks to me out loud!
Why would a young man not be proud
And tumble down, completely cowed,
    When such a one takes notice?

My legs are water under me.
My mind is a catastrophe.
I'm shaky in the third degree
    And helpless in his sight!

And yet I know a thing to do.
This martinet was feeble too
Until he learned whose bone to chew —
    As I can learn by heart!

The theme will touch on things of state:
"Though snakes are small, and dragons great,
Correct Ideas compensate."
Some day I'll eat from this man's plate.
    Li Ho will make the poem!

Spain, Summer, 1974
Dennis Lee

Ibn Amar Al-Andalusi, 1000 A.D.

The parks, the nights, the naked bodies' blur,
the fountains, and the library of course,
the olivetrees, the minarets, the myrrh,
the honeyed scent of joy without remorse.
He had a fair sword and a jet-black horse.
In pride he wrote this, because it was clear
that all within the high walls of Seville
worshipped and quoted him, the Grand Vizier:

"I am Amar. The fame of my verse flies
over the mountains and the western sea
and from the south and desert wind replies
only a fool is ignorant of me.
A golden lizard on a golden disc,
if I slither from the lewd lips of a boy
in the eager ear of an odalisque
she leaves her master and becomes my toy.
Nor will this change after my body lies
under my obelisk."

He was cheerful and happier than I
for when on Spanish domes the arabesque
loosened and fell, he never questioned why,
or why people grew flabby and grotesque,
and did not sense the fabric's fading dye
or in his own tunic the broken thread,
the fountains of the city running dry,
he did not taste the filth inside his bread
or see the boys who knew his poems die
or view the burning library with dread.
Brave and clever, he failed to note the fact
that faith's no help, nor wit, courage, or dagger
that no philosophy will resurrect
a culture, once it collapses forever.

Spain, Summer, 1974
George Jonas

Epitaph

He despised inane technologies,
decadence in contemporaries,
their machineries, their toys.
He shared their sufferings
but shunned their joys.

Toronto, 1975

Editor's Note

The originals of these poems were composed by George Faludy, the distinguished Hungarian poet and European man-of-letters, between 1935 and 1975. The translations were made by a group of writers, most of them Canadian, between 1967, when Faludy settled in Toronto, and 1976, when it became obvious that they should be collected and published. Five of the translators speak Hungarian, and these are: Andrew Faludy, the poet's son; Eric Johnson, a Toronto writer; George Jonas, the poet and playwright; Kathleen Szasz, a translator based in London, England; and Stephen Vizinczey, the essayist and novelist. None of the others knows the language. Four poets — R.G. Everson, Gwendolyn MacEwen, Raymond Souster, J. Michael Yates — made their translations from literal versions prepared by George Jonas. Jonas' own versions were completed in close consultation with the poet. Dennis Lee and I worked directly with the poet too. Lee's adaptations benefit for being highly characteristic of Lee's own writing; my own versions, the uncredited ones, being close transcriptions of the originals, were undertaken to communicate the poet's argument and imagery as much as to create original poems in English. Jonas' versions, being mid-way between these extremes of interpretation and literalism, probably express the fundamental Faludy most fully. All the translations published in this collection have received the poet's stamp of approval. (Needless to say, Faludy's own English — and French and German and Hungarian and Latin and Greek — are fluent and highly expressive.) Yet what is ultimately lost in *East and West,* which was compiled to demonstrate the range and development of forty years of Faludy's poetry, is the extreme playfulness of the original Hungarian: the innovative use of rhyme, the expressive rhythm, the unexpected insight, the rush of overpowering emotion, the sure sense of what makes a poem memorable and inevitable.

Notes on the Author
Biography

Faludy, George. Poet, writer. Born in Budapest, Hungary, Sept. 22, 1913. Educated at the universities of Berlin, Vienna, Graz, Paris, 1930-34. Second Lieutenant, Hungarian Army, 1934-35. Contributor to newspapers and periodicals, author of books, in Budapest. Sentenced for anti-Nazi activities to the State Prison, Budapest, 1936-38. Emigrated to Paris, 1938. Escaped from Paris to Morocco and interned in a camp at Ain Chock, near Casablanca, then at a camp in Marrakesh, 1940. With other European intellectuals, invited by Franklin Delano Roosevelt to settle in the United States, 1941. Honorary Secretary, Free Hungary Movement, 1941-46. Enlisted in the U.S. Army, 1942. Trained at Ft. Leonard Wood, Missouri. Served in the Pacific until 1945. Invited to return to Hungary and served as literary editor of *The Voice of the People,* Budapest, 1946-50. Arrested as a conspirator and as an American spy, 1950. Spent six months in the cellar of the Secret Police Headquarters, Budapest, summer and fall, 1950. Sentenced to twenty-five years hard labour at the camp at Recsk (a period described later in *My Happy Days in Hell*), 1950-53. Sentence then revoked. Worked in Budapest as a translator. Left Hungary in November 1956 at the time of the Revolution and settled in London, England. Editor-in-chief of the *Hungarian Literary Gazette,* 1957-61. Honorary Secretary of PEN's Centre for Writers in Exile, 1959-64. Immigrated to Canada and settled in Toronto, 1967. Taught at Columbia University, commuting to New York, 1968-71. Part-time lecturer — Wesleyan, Princeton, UCLA, University of Toronto, etc. — and freelance writer in Toronto.

Books

IN HUNGARIAN

The Ballads of Villon
(Poems after François Villon, Budapest, 1937; eleventh
edition, 1943, burnt by the Nazis; fifteenth edition, 1947,
confiscated by the Communists; twenty-seventh edition,
Stockholm, 1976)

At the Gates of Pompeï
(Poems, Budapest, 1938, burnt by the Nazis; second
edition, 1945, pulped by the Communists)

Heine's Germany
(Book-length poem, Romania, 1937, banned in Hungary;
second edition, Budapest, 1946, confiscated by the Communists in 1950)

An Anthology of European Poets
(Translations, Budapest, 1938; burnt by the Nazis, 1944;
second edition, 1946, confiscated by the Communists in
1950)

Laudatur
(Poems, Budapest, 1938; confiscated by the Communists
in 1948)

A Short History of Spain
(Book-length essay, Budapest, 1946)

The Dew of Autumn
(Poems, Budapest, 1947, pulped by the Communists)

A Keepsake Book of Red Byzantium
(Poems, London, 1961)

Letters to Posterity
(Selected poems, Toronto, 1975)

IN GERMAN

Tragödie eines Volkes
  (A short history of Hungary; Vienna,
  Zurich, Frankfurt, 1975)

IN ENGLISH

My Happy Days in Hell
  (Autobiography: André Deutsch, London, 1962; William
  Morrow, New York, 1963; Fremad, Copenhagen, 1964;
  Rutten und Loening, Munich, 1964; Didier, Paris, 1965)

Karoton
  (Historical novel: Eyre and Spottiswoode, London, 1966;
  William Morrow, New York, 1967)

Erasmus of Rotterdam
  (Biography: Eyre and Spottiswoode, London, 1970;
  Stein and Day, New York, 1971; Societas Verlag, Frank-
  furt, 1973)